EMPOWERED EVP

A SCHOOL OF HEALING AND IMPARTATION
WORKBOOK

COMPILED BY
RANDY CLARK

EMPOWERED: A SCHOOL OF HEALING AND IMPARTATION WORKBOOK

Unless otherwise noted, Scripture quotations are taken from HOLY BIBLE, NEW INTERNATIONAL VERSION®. Copyright © 1973, 1978, 1984 by International Bible Society. Used by permission of Zondervan Publishing House.

Scripture quotations marked (ESV) are from The Holy Bible, English Standard Version, copyright © 2001 by Crossway Bibles, a division of Good News Publishers. Used by permission. All rights reserved.

Scripture quotations marked (HCSB) have been taken from the Holman Christian Standard Bible®, Copyright © 1999, 2000, 2002, 2003 by Holman Bible Publishers. Used by permission.

Scripture quotations marked (ISV) are taken from the Holy Bible: International Standard Version®. Copyright © 2003 by The ISV Foundation. Used by permission of Davidson Press, Inc. ALL RIGHTS RESERVED INTERNATIONALLY.

Scripture quotations marked (NASB95) are taken from the NEW AMERICAN STANDARD BIBLE®, Copyright © 1960, 1962, 1963, 1971, 1972, 1973, 1975, 1977, 1995 by The Lockman Foundation. Used by permission.

Scripture quotations marked (Phillips) are taken from The New Testament In Modern English by J.B. Phillips Copyright © J.B. Phillips 1958, 1959, 1960, 1972 Macmillan Publishing Company.

Scripture quotations marked (RSV) Revised Standard Version of the Bible, copyright 1952 [2nd edition, 1971] by the Division of Christian Education of the National Council of the Churches of Christ in the United States of America. Used by permission. All rights reserved.

NOTE: Portions of some Scripture quotations have been bolded, italicized and/or underlined for didactic emphasis.

No part of this book may be reproduced, stored or transmitted in any form or by any means, electronic or mechanical, including photocopying and recording, or by any information storage or retrieval system, except as may be expressly permitted in writing by the publisher. For more information on how to order this book, requests permission, or for any of the other materials that Global Awakening offers, please contact:

Apostolic Network of Global Awakening

1451 Clark Street
Mechanicsburg, PA 17055
1-866-AWAKENING
globalawakeningstore.com

Sixth Edition, July 2022
© Copyright 2005, 2006, 2009 Global Awakening
All rights reserved

First Printing: August 2022
ISBN: 978-1-94-423815-5

TABLE OF CONTENTS

INTRODUCTION		3
Chapter 1	A FIVE-STEP PRAYER MODEL	5
Chapter 2	WORDS OF KNOWLEDGE	21
Chapter 3	THE BIBLICAL BASIS FOR HEALING	29
Chapter 4	SPEND AND BE SPENT	37
Chapter 5	HEALING AND THE KINGDOM OF GOD	41
Chapter 6	CHARISMATA THROUGH HISTORY 1	49
Chapter 7	CHARISMATA THROUGH HISTORY 2	63
Chapter 8	CHARISMATA THROUGH HISTORY 3	69
Chapter 9	DELIVERANCE: A NEW TESTAMENT REALITY	75
Chapter 10	THE BASICS OF DELIVERANCE	85
Chapter 11	DELIVERANCE: A TEN-STEP MINISTRY MODEL	93
Chapter 12	GROWING IN CONFIDENCE	103
Chapter 13	BREAKING FREE: PART 1	109
Chapter 14	BREAKING FREE: PART 2	113
Chapter 15	CESSATIONISM	123
Chapter 16	HEALING AND THE GLORY OF GOD	153
Chapter 17	HOW THIRSTY ARE YOU?	165

EMPOWERED EVP

INTRODUCTION

Empowered is a training school designed for the thirsty who desire to walk into higher realms of the supernatural. Our goal is to equip you with the knowledge you need to minister effectively in the areas of deliverance and disbelief.

On the first day, we will focus on THIRST. God has a destiny ready and waiting for you to step into. We will be teaching the basics of healing and illustrating the place healing has in modern day ministry. Each session will prepare you to walk in the healing power of the Holy Spirit, and one session will focus specifically on activating the spiritual gifts in you.

TRUTH is the topic of our second day. Church history is often a source of confusion, particularly when it comes to the charismata. In these sessions, you will have the opportunity to hear the truth behind the history of the charismata in the church and to learn more about ministering deliverance and healing.

The focus of the third day will focus on IDENTITY; to better equip you to walk in the power of the supernatural, we will show you how to overcome disbelief and solidify your identity in Christ. What God calls you to, He will empower, and you have a right to walk out and exercise that authority.

The final day of the school, ENCOUNTER, is specifically designed to be a hands-on course in healing and deliverance. Building on the lessons taught earlier in the school, these sessions will teach you about the importance of forgiveness in healing, how to break generational curses and soul ties, and further build your confidence in ministering healing and deliverance to those around you.

CHAPTER 1

A FIVE-STEP PRAYER MODEL

THE COMMISSION

Healing was central to the ministry of Jesus

Healing the sick was an integral part of the ministry of Jesus. Healing is mentioned in most places where the gospel speaks generally about His ministry. Matthew 4:23 is one example:

> **Matthew 4:23**
>
> Now Jesus went about all Galilee, teaching in their synagogues, preaching the gospel of the kingdom, and healing all kinds of sickness and all kinds of disease among the people.

Healing was part of Jesus' assignment to the twelve disciples:

> **Matthew 10:1, 5, 7-8**
>
> And when He had called His twelve disciples to Him, He gave them power over unclean spirits, to cast them out, and to heal all kinds of sickness and all kinds of disease… These twelve Jesus sent out and commanded them, saying, "… as you go, preach, saying, 'The kingdom of heaven is at hand.' Heal the sick, cleanse the lepers, raise the dead, cast out demons. Freely you have received, freely give."

And to the seventy:

> **Luke 10:1-2, 9**
>
> After these things the Lord appointed seventy others also, and sent them two by two before His face into every city and place where He Himself was about to go. Then He said to them, "...And heal the sick who are there, and say to them, 'The kingdom of God has come near to you.'"

Healing is part of the great commission assigned to all believers:

> **Mark 16:15-18**
>
> And He said to them, "Go into all the world and preach the gospel to every creature. He who believes and is baptized will be saved; but he who does not believe will be condemned. And these signs will follow those who believe: In My name they will cast out demons; they will speak with new tongues; they will take up serpents; and if they drink anything deadly, it will by no means hurt them; they will lay hands on the sick, and they will recover."

Therefore, ministering in the name of Jesus to the sick, with laying on of hands, is for "those who believe". This includes every member of the body of Christ!

Your Preparation

Preparation for ministry for the healing of others is very important.

Be a clean, clear channel for God to use!

Be "prayed up"! Pray a lot in tongues both before and during ministry time. If you don't pray in tongues, ask God fervently and specifically to be with you and to help you. He is the healer. If He doesn't come, the person you pray for won't get healed.

Take a moment to ask the Holy Spirit if there is anyone you need to forgive. If there is, forgive him or her at once from your heart. See Matthew 6:14-15.

Ask the Holy Spirit to show you any unconfessed sin in your life. If He does, repent sincerely at once and ask God's forgiveness for it. See Luke 13:2-5.

Ask God to give you His love for each person you pray for. Loving ministry will impact the sick person for good, whether or not his body is healed. He may not really know that God loves him. Your ministry may be his first experience of God's love.

Be aware that physical healing may take different routes. It may be instantaneous. It may come gradually in stages as you pray. It may come after repeated times of ministry. Or it may not come at all. God is sovereign. He heals when, how and whom He chooses in His own wisdom. Do not be put off if God does not heal someone you minister to. Our job is to pray. God is responsible for what does or does not happen.

Do not worry if the sick person does not seem to have faith for his healing. Faith helps, but God sometimes heals sick people who don't believe He can or will heal them - and sometimes when the one who prays does not have much faith either!

Be flexible. There is no universal rule about how to pray that will apply to all cases. There is nothing special in particular words. The Holy Spirit is the only sure guide. He may lead you differently from time to time. Practice listening to Him and following His leading.

The Holy Spirit may ask you to pray for something the person has not mentioned to you. In that case, include it in your prayer. Be clear, careful and tactful!

A FIVE-STEP PRAYER MODEL FOR HEALING

There are different ways of praying for the sick. The following Five-Step Prayer model is not the only one. If you have found one that is effective for you, use it in your own personal ministry.

This Five-Step Prayer model is used by Randy Clark and the ministry teams at Global Awakening crusades and events. It is quiet, loving and effective. It can be used by anyone.

The five steps are:

1. The Interview

2. Prayer Selection

3. Prayer Ministry

4. Stop and Re-interview

5. Post-prayer Suggestions

STEP ONE: THE INTERVIEW

Briefly interview the person requesting prayer. Be attentive and gentle; a loving attitude on your part will do much to reassure the person that he is in good hands. Ask him or her what the physical need is, but do not go into lengthy detail. For example:

- *"What is your name?" (A question or two to put the person at ease.)*
- *"What would you like prayer for?"*

- *"How long have you had this condition?"*
- *"Do you know what the cause is?"*
- *"Have you seen a doctor? What does he say is the matter?"*
- *"Do you remember what was happening in your life when this condition started?"*
- *"Did anything traumatic happen to you about the time your condition began or within a few months prior to it starting?"*

[You may need to explain why you are asking these last two questions.]

This is often sufficient for the initial interview. You may now know the nature and cause of the condition. In some cases you won't know and must ask additional questions, or simply ask the Holy Spirit for His leading. If His leading isn't clear to you, you must make an educated guess as to the nature and cause of the condition.

For example:

Perhaps there was an accident, which would usually suggest a natural cause. He may need to forgive the person who caused the accident. This could mean himself, if he caused it.

Perhaps he was born with the condition, which would often suggest a natural cause, or possibly a generational curse.

The condition may be partly or totally caused by emotional stress. Perhaps the person has had headaches ever since he lost a job. Maybe his back has hurt ever since someone cheated him. Or perhaps cancer was discovered a few months after a divorce, or after the death of a parent or child.

The cause might be spiritual. Perhaps the person has had nightmares ever since an occult experience he had. Maybe his condition is the result of a habitual sin, or perhaps the effect of a curse of some kind.

As noted above, if the cause is not known, ask the Holy Spirit for His leading as to the nature and possible cause of the condition. However, during your prayer for healing, you may want to consider other causes of the condition than the one you first considered, or you may want to go back to the interview stage and ask further questions (see the comments under Step Four on reinterviewing the person).

STEP TWO: PRAYER SELECTION

In the prayer selection, one must decide on the appropriate type of prayer ministry.

Types of prayer ministry:

Petition: A request to heal, addressed to God, to Jesus or to the Holy Spirit.

- *"Father, in the name of Jesus I ask you to restore sight to this eye."*
- *"Father, I pray in Jesus' name, come and straighten this spine."*
- *"Father, release Your power to heal, in Jim's body, in the name of Jesus."*
- *"Come, Holy Spirit. Release your power. Touch Jim's back, in Jesus' name."*

Command: A command addressed to a condition of the body, or to a part of the body, or to a troubling spirit such as a spirit of pain, or infirmity, or of affliction.

- *"In the name of Jesus, I command this tumor to shrivel up and dissolve."*
- *"In the name of Jesus, spine, be straight! Be healed!"*
- *"In Jesus' name, I command every afflicting spirit; get out of Jim's body."*
- *"In the name of Jesus, I command all pain and swelling to leave this ankle."*

A command is appropriate:

- *As your initial step, unless you are led otherwise by the Holy Spirit.*
- *When there has been a word of knowledge for healing or some other indication that God wants to heal the person at this time.*
- *When petition prayers have been tried and progress has stopped.*
- *When casting out an afflicting spirit or any other spirit.*
- *When a curse or vow is broken.*
- *Whenever you are so led by the Holy Spirit.*
- *As preliminaries to praying for healing.*

STEP THREE: PRAYER MINISTRY

First, audibly ask the Holy Spirit to come. You can say simply, "Come, Holy Spirit!" Or, "Come, Holy Spirit, with Your healing power." Or you may prefer a longer prayer. Then wait on Him for a minute or two.

Tell the person receiving ministry that you will be quiet for a minute or two, so that he doesn't become confused about what is going on.

An Attitude of Receiving

Ask the person not to pray while you are praying for him. Here again, be gentle and loving. Say something like: "I know this means a lot to you, and you have probably prayed a lot about your condition, but for now I need you to focus on your body. I want you to just relax and to let me know if anything begins to happen in your body, like heat, tingling, electricity, a change in the amount or location of the pain, etc. If you are praying in English, in tongues, thanking Jesus, or saying 'Yes, Yes!', it is harder for you to focus on your body. It is harder for you to receive healing."

Sometimes a person may find it very hard not to pray. Don't be hung up on this. Pray for him anyway.

If the presence of the Holy Spirit becomes evident, by the person feeling heat or tingling or some other manifestation, continue waiting on Him until He finishes what He wishes to do at that time. When the manifestation has ebbed, check to see if healing is complete. If it is not complete, continue your ministry.

Remember: always pray or command in the name of Jesus!

> **Mark 16:17-18**
>
> In my name ... they will lay hands on the sick, and they will recover.
>
> **Colossians 3:17**
>
> And whatever you do in word or deed, do all in the name of the Lord Jesus, giving thanks to God the Father through Him.

You cannot use the name of Jesus too much! The power is in His name. Some who have anointed healing ministries sometimes simply repeat "In the name of Jesus" over and over as their prayer for healing.

Thank God for whatever He does. You cannot thank God too much!

When you minister healing, seek to deal with the cause of the condition if you know the cause, as well as with the symptoms. For example:

- *"Father, in Jesus' name I ask you to heal the cones and rods in the retina of this eye. Father, in the name of Jesus, cause the scar tissue to dissolve and leave this eye. Oh God, restore the sight in this eye, in the name of Jesus."*

- *"In the name of Jesus, I command this ruptured disc to be healed and filled with fluid, and every pinched nerve to be released and soothed. In the name of Jesus, I command the pain to leave Joe's back."*

- *"In the name of Jesus, dear God, I ask You to heal this pancreas. Father, in the name of Jesus I ask You to touch this pancreas with your healing power and cause it to function normally. Cause it to produce insulin as needed and cause all diabetes to be cured and complete health restored. Release Your healing in the name of Jesus."*

- *"In the name of Jesus, I command every afflicting spirit and every spirit of infirmity, leave Joe's body, now!"*

- *"In Jesus' name I command all stiffness to leave this joint, all pain to leave and all swelling to subside. I command all calcium deposits and all scar tissue to dissolve in Jesus' name."*

- *"In Jesus' name, I command all chemical imbalances in Joe's body to be healed."*

- *"I command every organ furnishing chemicals or other signals to his organs to function normally in Jesus' name."*

Forgiveness of Another's Wrong Conduct

If it appears that someone else caused the condition or that someone wronged the person about the time the condition started, find out if the sick person has forgiven the other. If not, forgiveness should precede your prayer for healing. Unforgiveness can be a major obstacle to healing.

If you think forgiveness is called for, ask the sick person to forgive the other, even if the sick person is not aware of any resentment toward that person.

Examples:

- *A woman has had arthritis in her spine for five years, ever since her husband ran off with another woman. Has she forgiven her husband and the woman? Jesus said we must forgive, not we ought to. Emotional stress can cause illness and prevent healing. Sometimes one can be angry at God and must forgive Him.*

- *A pastor has had back pain for ten years. Ten years ago there was a split in his church and some of his closest friends turned against him. Has he forgiven the ringleaders of the split, his former friends, and all others involved?*

- *(Note: Sometimes a person is healed before you even begin to pray for healing, just by forgiving the person who caused the hurt, or just by repenting and asking God's forgiveness for his own sin of resentment and anger. The pastor noted above was healed by forgiving without any prayer for healing.)*

Repentance for One's Own Wrong Conduct and Asking Forgiveness for It

If it appears that the condition was brought on by sin, very gently inquire if the person agrees that this might be so. If he does, encourage him to repent and ask God's forgiveness. This should precede your prayer for healing. Sin that is not repented of can impede healing. Anger can contribute to back pain and some forms of depression. AIDS may result from a bad lifestyle choice. Lung cancer might have been caused by smoking.

Be tender. Ask if perhaps the condition could be related to his lifestyle. Perhaps say, "I wonder if this condition could be related to things you have done in the past." Never accuse the person confrontationally of causing his condition by his sin. It is seldom helpful and you may be wrong.

A caution: If this leading is of the Holy Spirit, the Holy Spirit will usually indicate the specific sin which is the problem, not sin in general. General accusations of sin are often destructive and probably are from the enemy.

A person may need to forgive himself. He may have caused his own injury or sickness. This may seem unnecessary, but sometimes it releases healing.

Some Practical Suggestions on How to Minister

If changes in the seeker's condition can be readily determined, it is appropriate and often helpful to pray short prayers or give brief commands interspersed with re-interviewing at frequent intervals to see if progress is being made.

- *"What has happened to the pain now?"*
- *"See if you can read the sign now."*
- *"Do you still feel heat in your stomach?"*
- *"Try moving your knee."*

A person may be partly or completely healed without feeling anything. He may not realize that healing has taken place until he uses the affected part. If he does something he could not do before or that caused pain before, he can see if the prayer thus far has made a difference.

When a prayer or command results in a partial healing, continue to use it until you find that it no longer produces further healing.

Two examples of short prayers with frequent interviews, in actual situations, are set out in Examples 1 and 2 at the end of this section.

Note that many of the prayers or commands for healing set out in scripture are very short.

- *"I am willing. Be cleansed." (Mark 1:41)*
- *"Little girl, I say to you 'Arise.'" (Mark 5:41)*
- *"God, be merciful to me, a sinner!" (Luke 18:13)*
- *"Please heal her, O God, I pray!" (Num. 12:13)*
- *"In the name of Jesus Christ of Nazareth, rise up and walk!" (Acts 3:6)*
- *"Jesus the Christ heals you. Arise and make your bed." (Acts 9:34)*
- *"Brother Saul, the Lord Jesus, who appeared to you on the road as you came, has sent me that you may receive your sight and be filled with the Holy Spirit." (Acts 9:17)*

If a long prayer is followed by partial healing, it is hard to know what part of the prayer or command was effective. Then, if it needs to be repeated, the entire prayer may have to be repeated.

Short prayers are not always called for, however. Where progress cannot readily be determined, such as with diabetes, frequent interviewing is not useful unless there are manifestations which help you to know what is going on. For example, if there is heat and the heat intensifies with certain prayers, then short prayers with frequent interviews may be appropriate.

Even if short prayers are appropriate, healing may not come after the short prayers. Healing will sometimes come after an extended time of prayer or after many prayers or after several times of praying.

Be Persistent

If you try one kind of prayer or command and get results, but not complete healing, continue. Explain why you are continuing to the person receiving prayer or he may wonder about the repetition. Be persistent!

If you try one kind of prayer or command and get no result after a few times, try another kind! Be persistent!

Sometimes a person expects you to pray only once for his condition and then stop. If he is not healed promptly, he may expect you to stop praying and he may start to leave. Encourage him to stay and let you pray more. Continue praying as long as God seems to be making any further change in his condition or as long as you are given different ways to pray for him. Be persistent!

If healing has partially come and then seems to stop, wait a bit. Continue praying for a time to see whether another wave of healing will come. Be persistent!

Your Manner

You need not necessarily pray aloud all the time. If you wish, tell the person that you may pray silently at times. As long as you have your hand on his arm, you are praying, even if not aloud. <u>Do</u> pray silently. Listen to the Holy Spirit. He may give you some guidance that you would otherwise miss.

It is often very helpful to pray with your eyes open and observe the person you are praying for. Look for signs that God is at work in his body: fluttering eyelids, trembling, perspiration. If you see something happening or if the person reports a change in the pain or increased sight or other progress, thank God for what He is doing and bless it. Continue to pray in the manner that led to the progress.

If you are not accustomed to praying with your eyes open, this will require practice! However, it is worth the practice as it sometimes helps you see what God is doing.

Use your normal tone of voice. Shouting or praying loudly in tongues will not increase your effectiveness.

Don't preach, don't give advice and don't prophesy.

STEP FOUR: STOP AND RE-INTERVIEW

If after a time you are making no progress, consider interviewing the person further.

Possible questions might be:

- *"Would you try again to remember whether anything significant happened within six months or so of the beginning of this condition?" (Some event may require forgiveness that the person may have forgotten or may have been unwilling to disclose.)*

- *"Do any other members of your family have this condition?" (If so, perhaps there is a generational spirit affecting several members of the family.)*

- *"Do you have a strong fear of anything?" (Fear can be a cause of many physical and spiritual problems and it sometimes interferes with healing.)*

- *"Is anyone in your family a member of the Freemasons or Eastern Star?" (Association with Masonic or other occult organizations is particularly likely to impede healing.)*

- *"Has anyone ever cursed you or your family that you know of?"*

- *"Have you had other accidents?" (If the person is accident-prone, consider whether he is under a curse.)*

- *"Have you ever participated in any kind of occult game or practice?"*

Consider whether a Wrong Spirit may be Present

If the person reports that the pain has moved or has increased, it signals the likely presence of an afflicting spirit. Simply command the afflicting spirit to leave in the name of Jesus. You might pray with more intensity, but not louder: "In the name of Jesus, I break the power of this afflicting spirit and command it to leave Joe's body" (or an equivalent prayer).

If the condition has existed a long time or if it is a condition that resists medical treatment, such as cancer, diabetes, Parkinson's, AIDS, etc, consider that there is likely to be a spirit causing the condition or resisting healing and command it to leave. "In the name of Jesus, I command any spirit of arthritis to leave this woman!"

When expelling a spirit of infirmity, an afflicting spirit or a spirit of a particular condition, a simple prayer may be enough. See the section on "Deliverance" for help in cases where expelling a spirit seems more difficult.

Inner Healing

Very often a person who requests prayer for a physical problem is also in need of emotional healing from hurts and wounds suffered as a result of trauma, physical or emotional abuse, perceived or real rejection, disappointments, fears, perceived or real inadequacies, and so on. These hurts and wounds may have accumulated over a long period of years.

Sometimes the physical healing of such a person cannot be fully realized unless and until his inner wounds and hurts have been healed or a process of healing begun.

Sometimes, even if a person seems to receive physical healing, it may be apparent that emotional healing is also needed.

Sometimes the person thinks his problem is physical, or sometimes you or he may think he needs deliverance. However, what he really needs may be inner healing.

In these cases, you should by all means take time to pray for the person's inner healing. Follow the leading of the Holy Spirit. Pray for the healing of hurts that have become apparent in your conversation with the sick person. If you are so led, inquire gently about the causes of the inner hurts. If circumstances permit, take time to understand the situations, at least in general. If time is limited, consider scheduling another session with the sick person.

Pray for the healing of each specific hurt just as you would for each specific physical ailment.[1] It is appropriate to inquire from time to time whether the Holy Spirit has put additional specific needs on the person's mind that you might pray for.

Allow the prayee to weep. Encourage it if he begins to cry. Let God love, comfort and console the person through you. When emotions are very strong, it is often helpful to ask Jesus to speak to the person or to show him how Jesus sees his situation. You may know other effective methods of praying for inner healing.

---

[1] Francis McNutt says specificity is particularly important in prayer for inner healing.

Ministry to a Person Who is Under Medical Care

You will have occasion to minister to people who are consulting with a counselor or psychiatrist. This probably is not a problem if your ministry is for a physical ailment, such as a broken limb or back pain. However, if healing for emotional problems is indicated, you should ask the prayee to get the approval of his doctor or counselor for his seeking prayer. This is especially important if the prayee is under medication.

Sometimes a person under medication, such as for diabetes, asthma, arthritis, heart disease, etc., believes he has been healed when you pray for him. He may think he can discontinue his medication. You must instruct him to continue his medication after your ministry to him; even if he believes and even if you believe he has been healed. He must return to his doctor and let the doctor change his medication if the doctor considers it appropriate to do so.

Ministry to a Person with Multiple Problems

As a general rule, it is better to finish praying for one condition before starting to pray for another unless the Holy Spirit directs you differently. Flitting from one problem to another is distracting. The person's faith will be built up for successive problems if one healing is completed.

The sick person may ask you to pray for a second problem as soon as you finish your first prayer for one condition. He may not understand that you will pray further for the first condition. Tell him gently that you will pray for the second condition, but first you wish to finish praying for the first condition.

Follow the leading of the Holy Spirit! If you are praying for a person's sinus infection and his bad foot begins to tingle, stop praying for the sinus condition and pray for the foot. Bless what God is doing and pray in cooperation with what He is doing. Go back to the sinus only when you have finished praying for the foot or when the sinus begins to manifest the presence of God at work there. Ask the Holy Spirit for His leading and expect to receive it.

Don't cause guilt in the person you are ministering to. Don't make him feel guilty if he does not get healed. Don't tell him it is his fault, even if you think it is!

If you think you may have made a mistake, don't fret over it. The Holy Spirit is bigger than your mistakes!

If possible, always use a catcher. A person may fall even though you are praying only for his physical healing. If you don't have a catcher, have the prayee sit down or stand against a wall so that he cannot fall or have the person stand in front of a chair so that he can settle into the chair if he becomes weak.

If the prayee falls, pray for him a few moments longer and then see if he has been healed ("How is the pain now?" "Try moving your neck now." etc.). Ask if he senses that the Holy Spirit is still touching him. If he senses that God is still at work in him, pray further for him. If nothing seems to be happening, ask the Holy Spirit whether you are through praying for him and continue as long as the Holy Spirit wants you to.

When to Stop Praying

Stop praying when:

- *The person is completely healed.*
- *The person wants you to stop. He may be tired or simply feel you should stop.*
- *The Holy Spirit tells you it is time to stop.*
- *You are not given any other way to pray and you are not gaining ground.*

STEP FIVE: POST-PRAYER SUGGESTIONS

After praying, consider the following:

Encourage the prayee's walk with the Lord.

You might share a scripture verse. For some people, scriptural passages are extremely meaningful and encouraging.

If a condition resulted from occult experiences or habitual sin, suggest tactfully that a change in lifestyle may well be needed to avoid a recurrence of his condition.

If he is not healed or not completely healed, don't accuse him of lack of faith for healing or of sin in his life as the cause.

Encourage the person to get prayer from others if there is little or no evidence of healing, or if his healing has not been completed. Encourage him to come back again for more prayer after the next meeting, etc. Sometimes healing is progressive and sometimes it occurs only after a number of prayers for healing have been made.

Tell the prayee not to be surprised if he experiences a spiritual attack after a healing. Help him to be prepared to resist it. If a symptom starts to recur, he can command it to leave in Jesus' name. If a bad habit is involved, he may be tempted for a short time to recommence the habit. If he does yield, quick repentance is needed and asking God's help to overcome.

Love! Love! Love!

> **1 Corinthians 16:14**
>
> Let all that you do be done with love.
>
> **1 Corinthians 13:4 RSV**
>
> Love is patient... kind... not jealous...not arrogant or rude.
>
> **1 Corinthians 13:4-5 Phillips**
>
> Love is not anxious to impress... not touchy.

As a minister of healing, do everything in love.

An Observation

If you pray for more people, you will see more people healed!

NOTES

NOTES

CHAPTER 2

WORDS OF KNOWLEDGE

LESSON GOALS

1. To answer the question, "What is a word of knowledge?"

2. To learn how to minister words of knowledge for healing.

3. To learn how to recognize when we are receiving words of knowledge - that is, how they may come to us or in what form we may receive them.

4. To examine practical insights for growing in the use of words of knowledge for healing.

5. To be activated in words of knowledge for healing!

INTRODUCTION

> **1 Corinthians 12:1, 7-8**
>
> Now concerning spiritual gifts, brethren, I do not want you to be unaware....But to each one is given the manifestation of the Spirit for the common good. For to one is given the word of wisdom through the Spirit, and to another the word of knowledge according to the same Spirit; (NASB95)

Our Heavenly Father, after the resurrection of Jesus Christ, sent to His children the person of the Holy Spirit with all of His fruit and gifts made available to us. In 1 Corinthians 12:7, Paul wrote that the manifestation of the Spirit is given for the **common good**.

In this lesson, we want to look at receiving **words of knowledge** for the release of healing. Notice this is an **activation clinic** session. At the end of the session, you will be given the opportunity to step out in faith to receive a word of knowledge for healing. This will be followed by the opportunity to pray for the individual that has the condition described in the word of knowledge you received. In your ministry to that person, you will use the Five-Step Prayer Model discussed in the previous lesson.

KEY INSIGHTS

What is a word of knowledge?

> **1 Corinthians 2:12-13**
>
> Now we have received, not the spirit of the world, but the Spirit who is from God, that we might know the things that have been freely given to us by God. These things we also speak, not in words which man's wisdom teaches but which the Holy Spirit teaches... (NKJV)

Simply, a **word of knowledge** is a supernatural revelation of information received through the Holy Spirit. It is knowledge received apart from natural analysis or human means.

Recognizing and Receiving A Word of Knowledge for Healing

How Does God Give a Word of Knowledge for Healing?

God gives His revelations in different ways. That is true of words of knowledge for healing, as well as for other kinds of revelation. Some of the more common ways He gives words of knowledge for healing are: Feel It, See It, Read It, Think It, Say It, Dream It, Experience It.

Let's look at each of these in detail.

Feel It

You may have: a sharp pain in some part of your body, a throbbing sensation, some other sensation, a strong emotion such as fear or panic.

Be careful that your feeling is not caused by a condition in your own body. For instance, if you often have pain in your left ear, you would not give that as a word of knowledge even if you get that pain during a meeting.

See It

You may get a mental picture, such as a body part: perhaps a heart, a foot, an eye, a head, a person with a certain condition such as a limp, a person carefully holding his arm, a crutch, eye-glasses, a person walking with a cane, a water bottle, a barbed wire fence, an auto accident.

Read It

You may see in your mind: a person with a word written across his front or back, or over his head, a word written on a wall or on a carpet, something like a newspaper headline, or a banner.

Think It

You may sense in your mind that someone has a particular condition, or that the Holy Spirit has spoken the word to you. It is a mental impression.

Say It

While talking or praying or standing with someone, unpremeditated words may tumble out of your mouth relating to a physical condition you were not aware of.

Dream It

While sleeping, you may have a vivid dream in which: you have a new health problem, you see someone with a health problem, you hear someone talking about a health problem, you see an event acted out before you like a move, such as a hospital scene or an accident.

Experience It

Similar to dreaming it, you may have a vivid vision while awake. It may be so strong that you are actually a part of what is happening, not just an observer.

Sometimes these categories blend together. Is it a mental picture or a vision? Vision could be likened to a "3D Technicolor movie" – something given by the Holy Spirit that is beyond a mental picture in intensity and vividness.

Ministering a Word of Knowledge for Healing

The Holy Spirit Gives a Word of Knowledge for a Specific Need

The Holy Spirit often gives a revelatory word of knowledge concerning the need of a person (or persons) for healing. This is an indication that God wishes to heal the person or those who have the condition revealed in the word of knowledge, and usually that He wishes to heal at the time the word is given.

When understood in this way, a word of knowledge builds faith in the person who needs the healing and also in the person who received the word of knowledge. Accordingly, the person who receives the word:

Should usually speak it out at that time or at the next appropriate time.

Should see if it applies to someone present, and if so, offer to pray at once for that person's healing.

The Context for Receiving a Word of Knowledge

You may receive a word of knowledge any time or anywhere.

You might get a word during a prayer meeting, a cell group meeting, walking past someone in church or in the supermarket, or while washing dishes at home.

You may or may not know for who the revelation is for.

Most often, the word of knowledge is given for someone present. However, it may not be for someone present, but for a person whom someone present knows about. Or it could be for someone you will see in the near future.

Expressing a Word of Knowledge for Healing and the Effect on Faith

The more specific the word of knowledge is, the more faith it builds in the people involved. If the word is received through feeling a pain, it is helpful to state the kind of pain and its exact location.

It is better to say, "A shooting pain on the left side of the neck just below the ear", or to point to the exact location, than to say merely, "A pain in the neck," or, "Does someone's neck hurt?"

Expressing a Word of Knowledge Only as Received

The person receiving the word should be careful not to change or add to it. When shared, it should not be exaggerated and no detail left out, even if it seems unimportant. Changes or additions cause confusion.

> ***Personal Illustration:*** *the man and the green hose. I once had a mental picture of someone being injured by tripping over a green hose. The only green hoses I had seen were garden hoses, so I said I had a picture of a person injured by tripping over a green garden hose. There was a man in the meeting who had been injured by tripping over a green pressure hose at work. He did not respond to my word at first, because the hose he tripped on wasn't a garden hose. He would have responded more quickly if I had not assumed that the green hose was a garden hose and had given it just as I had seen it.*

How to Deliver a Word of Knowledge for Healing

It is generally wise to be tentative in speaking out the word you have received.

For example, you might say, "Does anyone have a sharp pain in his left elbow right now?" If no one responds, don't be concerned. If someone responds, you could say, "Well, I just had a sharp pain in my left elbow, which may be a word of knowledge indicating that God would like to heal you now. Since you have that condition, would you like for me (or us) to pray for you now?"

If the person is open to receiving prayer, pray for him.

If he wants prayer later, pray for him later. If he doesn't want prayer due to embarrassment, lovingly encourage him to receive. But if he refuses, don't pressure him in any way to receive prayer.

Practical Insights for Growing in the Use of a Word of Knowledge for Healing

A word of knowledge may come quickly

Words of knowledge may come flitting through your mind more like a bird or dancing butterfly than like a stationary billboard.

A word of knowledge may be rather vague, tempting you to screen it out or to ignore it

Practice "tuning in" to these revelations and speaking them out. If you are tentative and humble, not arrogant or presumptuous, no one will be offended if you seem to have heard amiss.

Resist the thought that a word you have received is not important, or that it is "just you"

Remember, it builds faith in the other person to know that God has revealed that person's condition to you. What seems like a vague impression to you may be a shout to the other person! However, don't be presumptuous. Don't say, "God just told me you have an earache." Instead, say, "Does your left ear ever bother you? I have an impression of a problem in a left ear. Does this mean anything to you?"

Unpretentious honesty is the best policy!

It's perfectly okay: to admit that you're nervous, to say that you have only a vague impression, to say that you have never had a word for someone before, to say that praying for sick people is new to you.

Don't let fear rob you and the person who might have been healed

Someone has said that "faith" is spelled "r-i-s-k". Be patient, but step out! Be humble, but step out! Be tentative, but STEP OUT! God is giving you words of knowledge because He wants you to use them! He wants you to use them wisely and prudently and humbly, but He DOES want you to use them!

Activation

Now we get to the fun part! Again, if you have never received a word of knowledge, don't be afraid! Step out on the faithfulness of God and into the revelation of the Holy Spirit.

Remember:

- Gifts are given to us in the "Finished Work of Jesus Christ" in His atonement.
- Gifts are received by asking.
- Gifts are drawn to those who hunger and thirst for spiritual things.
- Gifts are received through faith, like everything else in the Kingdom.

My Personal History

I had been in the ministry 14 years without ever recognizing a word of knowledge.

I had both a B.S. degree in Religious Studies and a Master of Divinity degree from the School of Theology, but had no understanding of how to move in the gift of word of knowledge.

The very week I was told five ways you could have a word of knowledge I began having them.

One week later I taught on words of knowledge for the first time in my life. That very evening a woman had a word that led to a healing!

Ever since then every time I have taught on this subject, and given God the opportunity, there have always been people who receive their first words of knowledge. I have taught this teaching hundreds of times.

Today we shall see God be faithful once again, and at least 10% of this crowd who have never had a word of Knowledge will have their first word of knowledge. In a brief period of time I am going to pray and wait for 2 minutes during which time some of you who have never had a word of knowledge will have your first word of knowledge. I have never taught this when God didn't give people words of knowledge.

Of the ministry team on the bus in Brazil, one-half had NEVER had a word of knowledge or seen anyone healed. I told them that before 2 days were over they would all have a word of knowledge and pray for someone who would be healed. It happened then and has continued to happen!

SO, GET READY TO BE ACTIVATED!

NOTES

CHAPTER 3

THE BIBLICAL BASIS FOR HEALING

Christ the Healer
Barnum

Stand &, I'll say → "Bless you in the Name of Jesus"

LESSON GOALS

1. To gain a solid Biblical basis for the Ministry of Healing as it relates to:

    The Nature of God

    Messianic Prophecy

    Covenant, the Atonement and the Kingdom

    The Scope of Healing

2. To understand the Commission of healing to all *believers*.

3. To understand the Model of Humility, the Mystery and the Motivation of Healing as it relates to our moving in healing.

4. TO RECEIVE FAITH FOR HEALING AS THIS MESSAGE IS TAUGHT AND TO RESPOND TO THE ANOINTING OF GOD!

INTRODUCTION

In this lesson we make a brief journey through key Scriptures on the Biblical Basis of Healing. It is important in the ministry of healing to have a rock solid foundation as to the Father's will to heal. This way, no matter what we are faced with, we can move forward with full confidence that the Father desires to release healing through the name of Jesus, and in the power and anointing of the Holy Spirit.

> ***A Word of Preparation:*** *Today, while I am preaching the Word of God, God will heal people as they listen to the Word of God. I want you expecting to receive! When you feel the anointing, stand and remain standing until I see you and say, "God bless you in the name of Jesus." Then you may be seated.*

KEY INSIGHTS

The Self-Revelation of God – God is "The Lord that Heals"

In the book of Exodus, God reveals himself as Jehovah-Rapha, "the Lord who heals you". This name indicates the healing that flows out from the nature of God.

> **Exodus 15:26**
>
> He said, "If you listen carefully to the voice of the Lord your God and do what is right in His eyes, if you pay attention to His commands and keep all His decrees, I will not bring on you any of the diseases I brought on the Egyptians, for I am the Lord, who heals you."

Healing Would Be the Prophetic Indication for Recognizing the Messiah

Jesus confirms this by quoting Messianic prophecies in Isaiah chapters 35 and 61 in relationship to Himself and His ministry to the sick and demonized.

> **Isaiah 35:3-6**
>
> Strengthen the feeble hands, steady the knees that give way; say to those with fearful hearts, "Be strong, do not fear; your God will come, He will come with vengeance; with divine retribution He will come to save you." Then will the eyes of the blind be opened and the ears of the deaf unstopped. Then will the lame leap like a deer, and the mute tongue shout for joy. Water will gush forth in the wilderness and streams in the desert.

> **Isaiah 61:1-2a**
>
> The Spirit of the Sovereign Lord is on me, because the Lord has anointed me to preach good news to the poor. He has sent me to bind up the brokenhearted, to proclaim freedom for the captives and release from darkness for the prisoners, to proclaim the year of the Lord's favor...

> **Luke 4:18-19**
>
> "The Spirit of the Lord is on me, because He has anointed me to preach good news to the poor. He has sent me to proclaim freedom for the prisoners and recovery of sight for the blind, to release the oppressed, to proclaim the year of the Lord's favor."

> **Luke ~~7:18-19~~ 20-23**
>
> When the men came to Jesus, they said, "John the Baptist sent us to you to ask, 'Are you the one who was to come, or should we expect someone else?'" At that very time Jesus cured many who had diseases, sicknesses and evil spirits, and gave sight to many who were blind. So He replied to the messengers, "Go back and report to John what you have seen and heard: The blind receive sight, the lame walk, those who have leprosy are cured, the deaf hear, the dead are raised, and the good news is preached to the poor. Blessed is the man who does not fall away on account of me."

Every Christian Has Been Commissioned to Heal

Jesus very clearly stated that we as believers are commissioned to heal the sick. He taught and commanded His disciples to do so, and commanded them to pass it on to all believers.

> **Matthew 10:8**
>
> Heal the sick, raise the dead, cleanse those who have leprosy, drive out demons. Freely you have received, freely give.

> **Mark 6:7, 12-13**
>
> Calling the Twelve to Him, He sent them out two by two and gave them authority over evil spirits...They went out and preached that people should repent. They drove out many demons and anointed many sick people with oil and healed them.

> **Matthew 28:19-20**
>
> Therefore go and make disciples of all nations, baptizing them in the name of the Father and of the Son and of the Holy Spirit, and teaching them to obey everything I have commanded you. And surely I am with you always, to the very end of the age."

Luke 10:1 - 72 more Sent.
10:9 - Heal the sick the kingdom is at hand.

The Scope of Healing

> **Psalm 103:2-3**
>
> Praise the Lord, O my soul, and forget not all His benefits— who forgives all your sins and heals all your diseases.

THE BASIS FOR HEALING

The Covenant

In the old and new covenants, signs and wonders are part of each covenant.

> **Exodus 34:10**
>
> Then the Lord said: "I am making a covenant with you. Before all your people I will do wonders never before done in any nation in all the world. The people you live among will see how awesome is the work that I, the Lord, will do for you."

> **Hebrews 2:3-4**
>
> How shall we escape if we ignore such a great salvation? This salvation, which was first announced by the Lord, was confirmed to us by those who heard him. God also testified to it by signs, wonders and various miracles, and gifts of the Holy Spirit distributed according to His will.

The Atonement

Matthew 8:17 and I Peter 2:24 clearly relate the healing to the blood atonement of Jesus as prophesied in Isaiah 53.

> **Isaiah 53:4-5**
>
> Surely He took up our infirmities [sicknesses, Hebrew: "choli" – sickness, disease (noun form of chalah, to be sick or ill)] and carried our sorrows [pains, Hebrew: "makov" – pain], yet we considered Him stricken by God, smitten by Him, and afflicted. But He was pierced for our transgressions, He was crushed for our iniquities; the punishment that brought us peace was upon Him, and by His wounds we are healed.

> **Matthew 8:16-17**
>
> He drove out the spirits with a word and healed all the sick. This was to fulfill what was spoken through the prophet Isaiah:"He took up our infirmities and carried our diseases."

> **1 Peter 2:24**
>
> He himself bore our sins in His body on the tree, so that we might die to sins and live for righteousness; by His wounds you have been healed.
>
> **Acts 4:10**
>
> Then know this, you and all the people of Israel: It is by the name of Jesus Christ of Nazareth, whom you crucified but whom God raised from the dead, that this man stands before you healed.

THE KINGDOM

> **Luke 10:9**
>
> Heal the sick who are there and tell them, 'The kingdom of God is near you.'
>
> **Luke 17:21**
>
> "Nor will people say, 'Here it is,' or 'There it is,' because the kingdom of God is within you."

The Bible clearly relates the Kingdom to healing.

THE MODEL FOR HOW TO RESPOND TO HEALING – PETER'S HUMILITY

Peter was the first "non-stick, Teflon Christian" who let all praise "slide off" and gave all honor to the name of Jesus Christ for the healings.

> **Acts 4:9-10**
>
> If we are being called to account today for an act of kindness shown to a cripple and are asked how he was healed, then know this, you and all the people of Israel: It is by the name of Jesus Christ of Nazareth, whom you crucified but whom God raised from the dead, that this man stands before you healed.

THE MYSTERY OF HEALING

Greater and Lesser Degrees of Healing Anointing

Those in healing ministry must recognize that there will be times of greater and lesser degrees of anointing for healing.

At times the anointing is greater for healing:

The ministry of Jesus

> **Luke 5:17**
>
> One day as He was teaching, Pharisees and teachers of the law, who had come from every village of Galilee and from Judea and Jerusalem, were sitting there. And the power of the Lord was present for Him to heal the sick.

The ministry of Paul

> **Acts 19:11**
>
> God did extraordinary miracles through Paul…

At times the anointing is lower for healing:

The ministry of Jesus

> **Mark 6:4-6**
>
> Jesus said to them, "Only in his hometown, among his relatives and in his own house is a prophet without honor." He could not do any miracles there, except lay His hands on a few sick people and heal them. And He was amazed at their lack of faith.

Note: This is NOT meant as an encouragement to pass judgment when someone is not healed or the anointing is lower. This is to be discouraged (as discussed in the lessons The Five-Step Prayer Model and the Agony of Defeat). Our job is to press in for more! This just further illustrates that Jesus also operated in varying levels of anointing.

The ministry of Paul

> **2 Timothy 4:20**
>
> Erastus stayed in Corinth, and I left Trophimus sick in Miletus.

It is natural to want to ask why Paul, who "did extraordinary miracles", had not only little anointing, but apparently no anointing for the healing of Trophimus in Miletus. This illustrates our next point:

Not everyone is healed when you pray for healing

As discussed in the lesson, the Agony of Defeat, we must be able to say, "I don't know why some are healed and others are not."

In the face of defeat we must press on without blaming ourselves or the faith of those we minister to.

The Motivation for Healing – The Honor of the Name of Jesus!

In Ephesus, Paul stayed for two years and did extraordinary miracles in the name of Jesus (Acts 19:11). The Jewish exorcists using the name of Jesus were attacked and fled bleeding and naked after the demon had answered them, "Jesus I know, and I know about Paul, but who are you?" (Acts 19:15). As a result the people were seized with fear, "and the name of the Lord Jesus was held in high honor" (Acts 19:17b).

Our motive must ALWAYS be to honor the name of Jesus Christ. We also must be humble "Teflon" Christians following the example of Peter, who let glory from man "slide off" and give all glory to the name of Jesus Christ.

> **Acts 4:30**
>
> Stretch out your hand to heal and perform miraculous signs and wonders through the name of your holy servant Jesus.

Activation

Be prepared to give a word of knowledge or to participate in prayer ministry.

NOTES

CHAPTER 4

SPEND AND BE SPENT

LESSON GOALS

1. To recognize our need for transformation to enable us to reach the world.
2. Recognizing our need, to cry out with passion to receive a mighty impartation of the Holy Spirit.
3. To respond to the Holy Spirit's call to evangelism and world missions.

INTRODUCTION

> **2 Corinthians 12:15**
> So I will very gladly spend for you everything I have and expend myself as well. If I love you more, will you love me less?

The Story of Nobuo Tanaka: Still putting his life in the offering plate.

The purpose of this lesson is very simple:

- I want you to see the connection between the outpouring of the Holy Spirit and Missions and Evangelism.

- I want the Spirit to fall upon people, so that they fall under the power, but I also want people to get up and go to the lost and poor. Often revival breaks out among the young.

- I also want you to see the importance of Holy Communion in revival history.

KEY INSIGHTS

The focus of this lesson is rooted in two premises:

- **Premise 1**: We are too selfish to pay the price for powerful ministry unless we are touched by the Holy Spirit, who gives us boldness and the ability to live a more holy life.

- **Premise 2**: The most effective evangelism in the history of the Church has been through those who had such experiences of the Holy Spirit.

Illustrations from History and Contemporary Leaders

I want you to listen as I tell you the stories of those who have paid the price, of their desperate hunger, powerful Holy Spirit Baptisms, their transformation, and of the mighty revivals that have followed to transform nations.

Francis of Assisi

- *A Life Spent*

Ludwig Nicolaus Zinzendorf

- *200 yrs vs. 25 yrs*
- *100 Missionaries*
- *Moravian Motto: "To win for the Lamb that was slain the rewards of His suffering."*

John Wesley

- *Methodist revivals*

Evan Roberts

- *The Welsh Revival*
- *Age: 26*
- *His Spirit Baptism*

Sophal Ung: Cambodia

- *Anointed for Burial*
- *Underground Prison*

John G. Lake

- *12 men*
- *16 women & children*
- *500 churches in 5 years*

Luke Hubers

- *100,000 churches*
- *46 got his wish*

Heidi & Rolland Baker: Mozambique

- *Raygu*
- *Amori*
- *Surprise*
- *William*
- *Gun threats to pastors: "We're already dead men"*

Leif Hetland: Norway/Pakistan

- *1995 - Bulldozer for God in Muslim World*

IMPARTATION

This lesson will be followed by a time of impartation for the purpose of world evangelism and missions. These times are very powerful and many have been released into their destiny at these sessions.

NOTES

CHAPTER 5

HEALING AND THE KINGDOM OF GOD

LESSON GOALS

1. To understand the centrality of the Kingdom Message to healing and the Gospel.
2. To understand the impact of the "Kingdom now, not yet" on a theology of healing.
3. To understand the need for an integrated model of healing.
4. To consider what we can learn from former teachings within Protestantism.

INTRODUCTION

> **Luke 9:1-2**
>
> When Jesus had called the Twelve together, He gave them power and authority to drive out all demons and to cure diseases, and He sent them out to preach the Kingdom of God and to heal the sick.

In this passage in Luke's gospel, Jesus sent out the twelve to preach the kingdom of God and to heal the sick. In Matthew 6:10, He taught us to pray, "...your Kingdom come, your will be done on earth as it is in heaven." If we truly desire to "invade earth with heaven's realities" in the area of healing-or any other area, for that matter - then our understanding of the Kingdom, and a revelation of its nature, is crucial. In this session we want to take some time to ponder our perception, our view of the Kingdom of God and that view's influence on our faith for healing.

KEY INSIGHTS

The Kingdom Message is Central to the Gospel

John the Baptist preached that the kingdom of heaven was at hand:

> **Matthew 3:1-2**
>
> In those days John the Baptist came, preaching in the Desert of Judea and saying, "Repent, for the kingdom of heaven is near."

Jesus' message was centered on the Kingdom:

> **Mark 1:14-15**
>
> After John was put in prison, Jesus went into Galilee, proclaiming the good news of God. "The time has come," he said. "The kingdom of God is near. Repent and believe the good news!"

> **Luke 17:20-21**
>
> Once, having been asked by the Pharisees when the kingdom of God would come, Jesus replied, "The kingdom of God does not come with your careful observation, nor will people say, 'Here it is,' or 'There it is,' because the kingdom of God is within you."

> **Luke 18:17**
>
> I tell you the truth, anyone who will not receive the kingdom of God like a little child will never enter it."

> **Matthew 24:14**
>
> And this gospel of the kingdom will be preached in the whole world as a testimony to all nations, and then the end will come.

ethnos

Paul argued for and preached the Kingdom:

> **Acts 19:8**
>
> And he entered the synagogue and for three months spoke boldly, arguing and pleading about the kingdom of God; (RSV)

> **Acts 28:30-31**
>
> And he lived there two whole years at his own expense, and welcomed all who came to him, preaching the kingdom of God and teaching about the Lord Jesus Christ quite openly and unhindered. (RSV)

Philip preached the good news of the Kingdom of God:

> **Acts 8:12**
>
> But when they believed Philip as he preached good news about the kingdom of God and the name of Jesus Christ, they were baptized, both men and women. (RSV)

Healing and the Kingdom of God Message

This is not to be confused with Rushdooney's usage of the words "Kingdom now". It is grounded initially in the work of Baptist theologian George Eldon Ladd and popularized by professors at Fuller Theological Seminary.

The basic understanding of "Third Wave" proponents *[Kingdom now & not yet]*

- Popularized most by John Wimber and the Vineyard
- Other proponents: Dr. Charles Kraft, Dr. Derek Morphew, Dr. Don Williams, etc

Basic understanding of the "kingdom now – not yet," and its impact upon a theology of healing

This is the explanation for the question raised when some are healed and others are not. It has been my position for the last 20 years and I have taught it in my meetings. During 2005 I seriously began to question this position as far as its implications regarding healing. My concern was:

- In application it seems to be just one-half step behind seeing the healings as due to the sovereignty of God. God chooses to heal some and not others thereby leaving the onus of the problem on God, not man.

- This position seems to mitigate against:

    a. Praying through *[Pressing in]*
    b. Contending in prayer
    c. Praying fervently on behalf of the sick

In the circle of my experience at the Vineyard, there seemed to be little true expectation where:

a. there were no "words of knowledge" received.

b. there were no manifestations in the body of the person receiving prayer.

Faith expectation seemed to be based more upon a personal "word" than upon the promises of God in the Word of God. As I studied the writings and read the history of "healing movements" and the primary "healers" of those movements, I realized that their understanding of healing was:

a. Word based

b. Cross based

c. Gift/Anointing based

I also noticed that both the magnitude of the healings and the kinds of things healed were greater than in my own movement. Several years earlier I discovered that the truth was that everyone could move in the gifts and that everyone could receive words of knowledge and pray for the sick.

I have said this was a weakness and in the same sentence that this was a truth:

> The weakness was that there was such emphasis upon everyone receiving and the potentiality of being used for healing that there was little or perhaps no emphasis on the other scriptural truth that there are some in the Body of Christ that are "healers" and "workers of miracles". To say it another way, we allowed the pendulum to swing too far to one side, emphasis upon the situational gifting, in order to address an emphasis on the other side, the constituted gifting of those who had the calling as a "healer" or "worker of miracles."

As I traveled the world, I was meeting people who had been saved by their application of the teaching of the Faith Camp. I was made aware of pastors who were seeing major healings in their churches who had instructed their people in more of a "Faith Camp" position. In my reading I realized I had allowed Hank Hannagraaf to influence some of my opinions regarding faith camp leaders, especially E.W. Kenyon, and that Hank Hannagraaf had greatly misrepresented Kenyon. This was especially true in his connecting Kenyon to the "New Thought" influence from his training at Emerson College. I also came to see that E.W. Kenyon was influenced not by the "cults", but by the Holiness movement and by great Evangelical preachers like:

a. Baptist A. J. Gordon

b. A.B. Simpson- founder of the Christian Missionary Alliance and former Presbyterian minister

c. Andrew Murray – Dutch Reformed preacher and writer from South Africa whose books are still popular today

d. R. L. Stanton – former moderator of the Presbyterian Church *early pentecostal*

e. D. L. Moody, R. A. Torrey, and other great evangelical preachers of Kenyon's day

I noticed that Kenyon was credited as the major source for the understanding of healing for T.L. Osborne, who probably saw more people led to Christ and more healings than any other of the great healing revivalists of the famous 1948 healing revival.

The need for another emerging integrated model for healing

- Drawing upon insights from the "situational" gifting emphasis of the Vineyard, and its corresponding emphasis to train all the saints to pray for the sick.

- Drawing upon the older Pentecostal models of the constituted gifts of healing or the offices of "healers" and "miracle workers"

- Drawing upon the Latter Rain movement regarding the restoration of all the offices of the Apostolic Era and its emphasis upon training and releasing for healing and ministry within the local church.

- Drawing upon the emphasis of the Faith Camp in emphasizing the relationship between the Word of God and Faith. The Faith Camp today regarding healing is very similar to the "Faith Cure" movement of the late 1800's.

What can we learn from the former teachings that were positive regarding healing within Protestantism?

- Personal faith is important to the healing process.

- The Word of God is important for healthy faith.

- Avoid the negative view of medical healing. — *not a rule*

- A lack of faith may not be the only reason someone is not healed. We must learn from others that there can be root issues that are holding back the healing other than "lack of faith" or "sin in their lives."

- There is too much of an emphasis in the Church today upon the sovereignty of God which explains the lack of healings we do see.

Unity

- Our understanding of the authority delegated to believers needs to be stronger.
- What does, "... and the forceful lay hold of it by force," or "the Kingdom of God suffers violence and the violent lay hold of it" mean? Drawing upon the emphasis of the Faith Camp in emphasizing the relationship between the Word of God and Faith. The Faith Camp today regarding healing is very similar to the "Faith Cure" movement of the late 1800's.

Intimacy with God can overcome poor theology!

NOTES

NOTES

CHAPTER 6

CHARISMATA THROUGH HISTORY 1

LESSON GOALS

1. *In this and the following two lessons we will walk through Christian history examining the historical continuation of the Charismata.*

2. *In this lesson we will seek to understand the developments in the period up to 600 A.D.*

3. *We shall focus on the Topics Persecution and Purity, Plato, and Power.*

> **Mark 16:15-18**
>
> He said to them, "Go into all the world and preach the good news to all creation. Whoever believes and is baptized will be saved, but whoever does not believe will be condemned. And these signs will accompany those who believe: In my name they will drive out demons; they will speak in new tongues; they will pick up snakes with their hands; and when they drink deadly poison, it will not hurt them at all; they will place their hands on sick people, and they will get well."

> **2 Timothy 3:1-5**
>
> But mark this: There will be terrible times in the last days. People will be lovers of themselves, lovers of money, boastful, proud, abusive, disobedient to their parents,
>
> ungrateful, unholy, without love, unforgiving, slanderous, without self-control, brutal, not lovers of the good, treacherous, rash, conceited, lovers of pleasure rather than lovers of God— having a form of godliness but denying its power. Have nothing to do with them.
>
> **2 Timothy 3:1-5**
>
> The Spirit clearly says that in later times some will abandon the faith and follow deceiving spirits and things taught by demons.

In the introduction to Dr. Morton Kelsey's book, Healing and Christianity, which was published in 1973, he writes:

> *Finally, in the past 30 years or so men in other areas of medicine have come to realize that many physical illnesses can have a psychic factor....With growing realization that man cannot be treated piecemeal, physicians have begun to treat him as a whole functioning organism, including his social and religious life...*[1]

> *But the average "orthodox clergyman is not much interested in practices that would convey healing. The "orthodox" Christian, whether liberal or conservative, has little exposure to such sacramental acts and little or no interest in physical or mental healing through religious means..."* [2]

Kelsey follows with examples where doctors and clergy were called together to discuss spiritual healing. The physicians were actively interested, but the clergy were indifferent or didn't even take the topic seriously. He then continues:

> *What, then, is the place of healing in the Christianity of the modern world? ...difference over the value of sacramental or religious healing in the church is only one symptom of a fundamental division among Christians about how God acts in human life. The points of view are so diametrically opposed and so deeply divided that they are often unspoken, and each side simply accepting the validity of its own view without question.*

Thus in the Christian churches today we find two conflicting attitudes toward the ministry of healing of Jesus of Nazareth and the apostles – a ministry that was practically unbroken for the first thousand years of the church's life. On one hand, among certain religious groups today we find an increasing interest in this spiritual ministry of healing. On the other, we come face to face with the fact that in most Protestant churches today there is actual hostility to the practice of religious healing-hostility even to the idea of it.[3]

Kelsey follows with three key questions:

- "How has the church become so divided?"
- "Which point of view is nearer the heart of a vital Christianity?"
- "Which attitude fits better the knowledge of man and his world?"[4]

The answer to those three questions is the purpose of this three-part teaching.

How did the Church which witnessed so much healing its first thousand years of life begin to lose this vital powerful ministry?

How did Protestantism become so closed to the ministry of healing, especially from its beginning in 1517 until the middle to late part of the 19th Century?

Only after the emergence of Pentecostalism was Protestantism truly affected in a significant way, reversing its anti-healing position.

These lessons are to help us understand how the traditional protestant church and its members became so opposed to the ministry of healing within its services.

This topic is divided into three significant periods in the life of the Church, and each reveals the reasons for success and/or failure in the healing ministry.

KEY INSIGHTS

Persecution, Purity, Plato and Power (30-600 A.D.)

Persecution and Purity

Notice three things about Persecution:

- Persecution came from the Christian threat to the status quo.
- Persecution produced Purity.
- Persecution prevented lukewarm, nominal believers.

The following information on Persecution has been extracted and condensed from Study 9 THE CHURCH IN PERSECUTION: Sell, H. T. (1998, c1906). Studies in early church history. Willow Grove, PA: Woodlawn Electronic Publishing. Copyright, Public Domain:

Jewish Persecution

The persecutions began in Jerusalem, with the crucifixion of Christ; they continued after His resurrection when the Jews hauled the apostles before the magistrates and in imprisoning them for speaking and teaching in His name (Acts 4:1–21; 5:18–42). They broke out afresh upon the martyrdom of Stephen led by Saul (Acts 7:52-60; 8:1-4). When Saul was converted, the Jews never ceased to harass him in every city in which they were strong enough to do so.

The time of the persecutions of the Jews was, however, quite limited. After 70 A.D. they ceased to be of much consequence, not because the bitterness of their spirit was taken away, but because their power to do harm was seriously weakened through the destruction of their holy city.

Roman Persecution

An attempt was made by the Romans to bind their people together by a religion. The necessity of a universal religion was felt in the face of the political unity, which had been accomplished by force of arms. The unity of the state required a common religion to create a common tie amongst the heterogeneous populations. This universal, made-to-order political religion was an eclectic one, a patchwork, taking elements from this and that national religion with a deified emperor at the head to whom was paid divine honors. It was a religion in which vice - in "the mysteries" - often clothed itself in the mantle of worship and made religion its servant; hence the awful immoralities prevalent in society of which Roman writers tell us.

The worship of the Roman emperor was the one form of worship, however, which was coextensive with the empire. Not to worship the image of the emperor was considered an act of treason to the state.

At first the Romans did not persecute the Christians because they were not awake to the radical nature of their teachings. Christianity was supposed to be a sect of Judaism and Judaism was a national religion and under the protection of the empire. The Jews took the same stand as the Christians against the worship of the emperor as a god, yet this was not made a ground of accusation and persecution, because Judaism was practically limited in its scope to the Jews. Had the Christians been willing to take its place with a hundred or so of other religions, there would have been no persecution, but it claimed to be the one true faith. The Christians were guilty of a double offense - they strove by every means to persuade citizens to abandon the worship sanctioned by Roman law and to introduce rites not sanctioned by it.

The scope of the persecutions was coextensive with the empire. The time was about three hundred years from Christ to the Emperor Constantine.[5]

Plato and His Dualistic Philosophy

Plato believed in a Dualistic nature of reality. In his worldview the physical world was a shadow of the greater reality of the spirit realm. According to Kelsey:

> *Platonic philosophy tried to show how the tangible world, of which man's body is a part, constantly interacts with a world of Ideas, spirits, demons, and deities. In this framework*

the Old Testament descriptions of man's direct dealings with God made good sense, as did the dreams and visions, the healings, prophecies, and angels and demons of the New Testament.[6]

In Dualism, the spirit realm is superior, valuable and good, but the natural realm is inferior, worthless and even evil. This Dualistic Platonic worldview and philosophy later manifest itself in the Neo-Platonism and Gnosticism of the New Testament period.

Why this is important for our discussion

The influence of the Dualism of Platonism had both a positive and negative effect:

- The Positive: Those who held a Platonic worldview believed in an active eternal spirit realm which affected and influenced the natural world, thus opening them up to the message of the gospel of Jesus the Victor who triumphed over the powers of darkness and evil.

- The Negative: Those who held a Platonic worldview devalued the physical realm, including the human body. This contrasts with the Biblical and Hebrew view, which has at times manifested in the extremes of asceticism and licentiousness, and has affected the acceptance or rejection of the healing ministry through the course of Church history.

Power: The Testimony of Healing in Early Church History

We will now consider reliable witnesses from early Church history who witnessed and/or participated in healing ministry. [The information in this section is drawn almost exclusively from quotations of Morton T. Kelsey's Healing and Christianity, as referenced in the endnotes.]

The Testimony of the Anti-Nicene Fathers

All of these lived after the Apostles had died and some of them after the Bible was canonized, which historically disproves cessationism.

a) Justin Martyr (100-165, martyred in 165 A.D.)

Justin Martyr wrote in his "apology" addressed to the Roman emperor:

> *For numberless demoniacs throughout the whole world, and in your city, many of our Christian men exorcizing them in the Name of Jesus Christ...have healed and do heal, rendering helpless and driving the possessing devils out of the men, though they could not be cured by all the other exorcists, and those who used incantations and drugs.*[7]

Justin Martyr tells in several places how Christians healed in the name of Jesus Christ, driving out demons and all kinds of evil spirits. Writing about the charismata, the gifts

God pours out upon believers, he calls attention to the power to heal as one of the particular gifts that was being received and used.[8]

b) Hermas (Died c. 150)

From the Shepherd of Hermas one can see the strong emphasis that was on the ministry of healing in the early Ante-Nicene church. Hermas wrote:

> "He therefore, that knows the calamity of such a man, and does not free him from it, commits a great sin, and is guilty of his blood." Indeed the healing of physical illness was seen in this period as telling evidence that the Spirit of Christ was actually present and at work among Christians. Since both bodily and mental illness were a sign of domination by some evil entity, the power to heal disease was prime evidence that the opposite spirit –the Spirit of God – was operating in the healer. Thus the healing of "demon possession" was often spoken of in conjunction with curing illness from other causes.[9]

c) Tertullian (160-225)

In a telling protest written to the proconsul in North Africa during the persecutions there, Tertullian cited facts even more specifically:

> All this [that is, the number of times Roman officials simply dismissed charges against Christians] might be officially brought under your notice, and by the very advocates, who are themselves also under obligations to us, although in court they give their voice as it suits them...And how many men of rank (to say nothing of common people) have been delivered from devils, and healed of diseases!

It was simply a fact of Christian experience which pagan officials could verify if they wished. Tertullian, explicitly identified persons who had been healed and testified to their great number and the wide range of physical and mental diseases represented. Elsewhere he also says that God could, and sometimes did, recall men's souls to their bodies.[10]

d) Origen (185-254)

Origen wrote his great treatise, *Against Celsus*, to take pagan thinking apart piece by piece, and here he spoke in several places of how Christians "expel evil spirits, and perform many cures" - many of which he had himself witnessed. Or again, "the name of Jesus can still remove distractions from the minds of men, and expel demons, and also take away diseases." Several such statements occur in this work, which was written especially for the top-level pagan community. Cyprian told in one of his letters how baptism itself was sometimes the means by which a serious illness was cured, and that there were Christians living on and giving their lives to the church because of such an experience.[11]

e) Quadratus

Quadratus, who wrote an apology presented to the emperor Hadrian stated that the works of the Savior had continued to his time and that the continued presence of men who had been healed left no question as to the reality of physical healing.[12]

f) Theophilus of Antioch (died c. 181)

Theophilus of Antioch specified the physical healing of human beings he had witnessed as particular evidence that the resurrection was beginning to work in them and death being put to flight; he also spoke of the fact that demons were sometimes exorcised and confessed their demonic nature.[13]

g) Eugenia

In the Acts of Eugenia, where she is portrayed as being so close to God that she could cast out devils. It is told how a certain noblewoman of Alexandria was healed of a recurring fever when Eugenia prayed over her.[14]

h) Minucius Felix (Second century)

Minucius Felix in the dialog Octaviu, one of the earliest Latin apologies, written about the end of the second century, describes the exorcism of demons in these words:

> *Since they themselves are the witnesses that they are demons, believe them when they confess the truth of themselves; for when abjured by the only and true God, unwillingly the wretched beings shudder in their bodies, and either at once leap forth, or vanish by degrees, as the faith of the sufferer assists or the grace of the healer inspires.*[15]

i) Irenaeus (flourished c. 175-195)

Perhaps the most interesting discussion of healing among the ante-Nicene fathers came from Irenaeus in Gaul. In Against Heresies, one of his telling points was that heretics were not able to accomplish the miracles of healing that Christians could perform. Irenaeus attested to almost the same range of healings as we have found in the Gospels and Acts. All kinds of bodily infirmity, as well as many different diseases, had been cured. The damage from external accidents had been repaired. He had seen the exorcism of all sorts of demons. There is no indication that Irenaeus viewed any disease as incurable or any healing as against God's will. Indeed the whole attitude he voiced was that healing is a natural activity of Christians as they express the creative power of God, given them as members of Christ. In one place Irenaeus speaks of the prayer and fasting of an entire church as effective in raising a person from the dead.[16]

j) Arnobius and Lactantius

Near the end of the ante-Nicene period, from 300- 325, Arnobius and Lactantius, his pupil, wrote about healing. Lactantius wrote about what he had witnessed in the church in his time. He wrote,

> *As He Himself before His passion put to confusion demons by His word and command, so now, by the name and sign of the same passion, unclean spirits, having insinuated themselves into the bodies of men, are driven out, when racked and tormented, and confessing themselves to be demons, they yield themselves to God, who harasses them.*[17]

The Testimony of the Doctors of the Church

The doctors of the Church refers to a small group of men who had a profound impact upon the development of what would later be considered "orthodoxy". These were among the most brilliant and strongest leaders of the early Church. Most were born a few years before or sometime after the Edict of Milan in 313, which gave Christianity the status of a legal religion. Only a few years later, Christianity would become the official religion of the Roman Empire. There would be many heresies to face and the church would be wrestling with its faith, but we shall see that healing continued to be very important to this faith.

Doctors from the East

We shall consider four men from this group. The first, Athanasius, was the main defender of the Trinitarian understanding of the Christian faith. The other three, called the great Cappadocians, were Basil the Great, his brother Gregory of Nyssa, and their friend, Gregory of Nazianzus. The life and power of Gregory Thaumaturgus (called the "Wonder Worker") who came to Cappadocia in the days of Persecution, strongly influenced the families of these three.[18] The greatest preacher of the time, John Chrysostom (345-407), who was known as "the Goldenmouth" for his eloquence popularized their ideas.[19]

Athanasius (296-393)

Athanasius was the main defender of the Trinitarian understanding of the Christian faith. He and four other Eastern theologians all wrote about healing occurring during their time. These were five of the most intelligent, spiritual, leaders of the Church during this time. Together they were used to forge the orthodoxy of the early Christian doctrines. These are doctrines that have changed little in the East since their time.

Gregory of Nazianzus (329-396)

Gregory of Nazianzus became the bishop of Constantinople after the Arian controversy. The historian Sozoman tells of how Gregory was used in the healing of a pregnant woman. In the account he writes, regarding the Orthodox church, "The power of God was there manifested, and was helpful both in waking visions and in dreams, often for the relief of many diseases."[20]

According to Gregory's brother Caesarius, who was noted for his brilliant medical career, "In place after place Gregory showed his understanding of the 'deep roots' of disease and how closely the church's task with people was allied to the job of the medical practitioner."[21]

Gregory tells of two healings from his immediate family:

- His sister was dragged by a team of mules and was so hurt that no one thought she would live. She was saved by the prayers of the congregation. She was healed again years later when she developed a terrible disease. She had an extremely high fever and had comatose-like experiences. The physicians couldn't help her. She was healed when she went into the church and took the "bread of the Presence", the Eucharistic bread, and rubbed it all over her body.[22]

- Gregory's father, also a Bishop was healed through the prayers of the church. This great family was certainly not a stranger to the healing ministry for they experienced it in their own immediate family. His healing was associated with the celebration of the Mass. His mother was healed through a spiritual dream.[23]

Basil the Great (329-379)

Basil founded what was probably the first Christian hospital, located outside Caesarea. He saw no conflict between faith and healing. Basil answered the question, "whether recourse to the medical arts is in keeping with the practice of piety." He believed that medical science had been given to men by God to be used when necessary, although not as the only decisive factor. He stated, "to reject entirely the benefits to be derived from this art is the sign of a petty nature."[24]

Two healings from Basil's ministry were recorded by Gregory of Nazianzus:

- The first occurred when he (Basil) was about to be exiled by the emperor Valens, whose small son was suddenly sick and in pain. When physicians could not help the baby, the emperor had a change of heart and called for Basil, who came immediately. According to the reports of those present, the boy began to improve at once, but later died because his father was overanxious and asked the physicians to try their treatment again.[25]

- The other incident also occurred during a personal conflict, this time with the Bishop Eusebius, who was then taken ill and called for him. He went willingly, and Eusebius confessed that he had been in the wrong and asked to be saved. According to Gregory, his life was indeed restored, and Eusebius never ceased to wonder at Basil's power.[26]

Gregory of Nyssa (331-396)

Gregory of Nyssa was the only one of the Eastern theologians who, concerning healing, made a definite statement relating it to his total theology. In The Great Catechism and On the Making of Man, his key works, he describes healing as the main door through which a knowledge of God reaches men.[27] He recorded in great detail a number of healings witnessed by others including the healing of a lame Roman soldier's limb as he cried out in prayer at a shrine, and a healing by the prayer of a woman known as St. Macrina of a child losing sight from a severe eye infection.[28]

Doctors from the West

There were four men in the western part of the Roman Empire who were later recognized as Doctors of the church. They were Ambrose (340-397), Augustine (354-430), Jerome (340-420) and Gregory the Great (540-60?). All of these men wrote about healings in their day, but because they viewed it differently, this set the stage for changes in the church.

Two other men need to be mentioned from this time period: John Cassian, who was responsible for laying foundations for the monastic movement in the West, and St. Martin of Tours and his biographer Sulpitius Severus. St. Martin of Tours was noted as one of the great wonder workers of the Catholic Church of the west during this time.

The Testimony of Ancient Historians

There were four historians of the first 600 years of Christianity and all of them include accounts of healing during the whole of this period. They were: Eusebius, the first historian of the church. He was a contemporary of the Emperor Constantine who legalized Christianity in 313 A.D. with the Edict of Milan. He was followed by the historians, Sozomen, Socrates Scholasticus, and Theoderet. Socrates, for instance, tells how Maruthas, the Bishop of Mesopotamia, cured the Persian king of headaches which the Magi had not been able to relieve, and that Maruthas was permitted in consequence to establish churches wherever he wished in Persia.[29]

What a great example this was of what we today would call "Power Evangelism". We will see more examples of the connection between power to heal and deliver and the missionary expansion in the Church.

The Testimony of Augustine

Augustine was the undisputed theologian in the west for 1,000 years. His influence is very important to the history of healing. In his early years of ministry he wrote critically of healing. He wrote:

> *These miracles are not allowed to continue into our time, lest the soul should always require things that can always be seen, and by becoming accustomed to them mankind should grow cold towards the very thing whose novelty had made men glow with fire.*[30]

However, about 40 years later he corrected this view which seemed to be antagonistic towards the on-going ministry of healing in the Church. He wrote in his last and greatest work, The City of God, completed in 426, a whole section that gave high value to the ongoing ministry of healing. In this section he noted that over 70 healings had been recorded in his own bishopric of Hippo Regius in 2 years. He stated in his Revisions:

> *"It is indeed true: that not everyone today who has hands laid on them in baptism thus re-*

ceives the Holy Spirit so as to speak in tongues; nor are the sick always healed by having the shadow of the promise of Christ pass across them; and if such things were once done, it is clear that they afterwards ceased.

But what I said should not be taken as understanding that no miracles are believed to happen today in the name of Christ. For at the very time I wrote this book I already knew that, by approaching the bodies of the two martyrs of Milan, a blind man in that same city was given back his sight; and so many other things of this kind have happened, even in this present time, that it is not possible for us either to know of all of them or to count up all of those that we have knowledge of."[31]

Dr. Morton Kelsey asks, "What had happened to change his view?" and traces the story from Augustine's writings, sermons and biographical material. It begins in 415 with the discovery of the bones of the martyr Stephen. Some of these relics were brought to his church. In 424, two weeks before Easter, as he was preparing to conduct the services, a young man who was troubled, both he and his sister, with convulsive seizures was suddenly healed. How did this happen? For two weeks this man and his sister had came to the reliquary in the sanctuary of Augustine's church to pray for healing. On this day, the young man was praying as he was holding onto the screen of the reliquary. Suddenly, he fell down as if dead. Augustine was in the vestibule preparing for the processional. The people were frightened by the fall of the young man and feared he had died. Suddenly, the young man rose to his feet staring back at the crowd of people. It was apparent to all that he had been healed. He now was normal. Augustine had the young man stay after the meeting to have dinner with him so they could talk.

On the following days Augustine preached about St. Stephen, the healing, and also other martyrs and healings. On the third day after Easter he read the young man's statement, while both brother and sister stood on the choir steps where the whole congregation could see them – one quite and normal, the other still trembling convulsively. Augustine then asked them to sit down, and was giving his sermon about the healing when he was interrupted by loud cries. The young woman had gone straight to the shrine to pray, and exactly the same thing had happened to her. Once more she stood before the people, this time healed, and in Augustine's own words, 'Praise to God was shouted so loud that my ears could scarcely stand the din. But, of course, the main point was that, in the hearts of all this clamoring crowd, there burned that faith in Christ for which the martyr Stephen shed his blood.' In this last section of his final great work Augustine paid his dues, all at once, to the reality of healing. It was one of the ways, he now saw, that men find how true the gospel really is, particularly the resurrection.[32]

Augustine was aware not only of the many healings which occurred in his bishopric over a two year period, he was also aware of other bishops with whom he communicated that were also having healings in their areas.

Before Augustine died he became known for the healing anointing and authority to deliver flowing through his own life. A major healing occurred during Augustine's own illness. It occurred after his completion of *The City of God*, while Hippo was under siege.

His biographer Possidius tells us the story:

> *A certain man came with a sick relative and asked him to lay his hand upon him that he might be cured. Augustine replied that, if he had any such power, he certainly would have first applied it to himself. Thereupon, his visitor replied that he had had a vision and in his sleep had heard these words: "Go to Bishop Augustine, that he may lay his hand upon him, and he will be healed!" When Augustine learned this, he did not delay doing it and immediately the Lord caused the sick man to depart from him healed.*[33]

Possidius also tells us that Augustine prayed with tears and supplication for certain demoniacs freeing them from their possession.

Augustine would have a tremendous affect upon the thinking and writing of the Reformers Luther and Calvin. Augustine's strong view of predestination and his writings regarding God's sovereignty would change the view of the early church from a "Warfare Worldview" to the "Blueprint Worldview." This would ultimately have a very negative impact upon the theology of healing for the history of the Church.

Endnotes

[1] Morton T. Kelsey, Healing and Christianity [New York, NY: Harper and Row, Publishers, 1973, 1976 (paperback)] p. 5

[2] Ibid. p. 6

[3] Ibid. p. 6

[4] Ibid.

[5] The information on Persecution has been extracted and condensed from Study 9 THE CHURCH IN PERSECUTION: Sell, H. T. (1998, c1906) Studies in Early Church History (Willow Grove, PA: Woodlawn Electronic Publishing, Copyright, Public Domain)

[6] Morton T. Kelsey, Healing and Christianity [New York, NY: Harper and Row, Publishers, 1973, 1976 (paperback)] p. 139

[7] Ibid p. 136, Kelsey references: (Justin Martyr, Second Apology to the Roman Senate 6: see the Anti-Nicene Fathers)

[8] Ibid. p. 149

[9] Ibid. p. 149

[10] Ibid. pp. 136-137

[11] Ibid. p. 136

[12] Ibid. p. 149

[13] Ibid. p. 149

[14] Morton T. Kelsey, *Healing and Christianity* (New York, NY: Harper and Row, Publishers, 1973, 1976) p. 159

[15] *Ibid. pp. 150*

[16] *Ibid. pp. 150-151*

[17] *Ibid. p. 152*

[18] *Ibid. p. 173*

[19] *Ibid. p. 160*

[20] *Ibid. p. 169*

[21] *Ibid. p. 168*

[22] *Ibid. p. 168*

[23] *Ibid. pp. 168-169*

[24] *Ibid. p. 167*

[25] *Ibid. p. 168*

[26] *Ibid. p. 168*

[27] *Ibid. p. 174*

[28] *Ibid. pp. 172-173*

[29] *Ibid. p. 162*

[30] *Ibid. p. 185, Kelsey references: (De Vera Religione, cap. 25, nn. 46, 47)*

[31] *Ibid. p. 185, Kelsey references: (De Vera Religione, cap. 25, nn. 46, 47)*

[32] *Ibid. pp. 186-187*

[33] *Ibid. pp. 187-188*

NOTES

CHAPTER 7

CHARISMATA THROUGH HISTORY 2

LESSON GOALS

1. In this lesson we will continue our walk through Christian history examining the historical continuation of the Charismata.

2. In this lesson we will seek to understand the developments in the period up to 430 A.D to 1900.

3. We shall focus briefly on three periods:

    - *Disaster, Decline, Distortion and Desert Divines (430-1200 A.D.)*

    - *Arab, Aristotle and Aquinas (1200-1517 A.D.)*

    - *Scholasticism, Skepticism, Scofield and Sanctification: (1517-1900 A.D.)*

INTRODUCTION

In the previous lesson, we set down a detailed survey concerning the supernatural legacy of healing in church history through 430 A.D. It was essential for this and the next lesson that we establish a solid base of thought upon which to build. To understand the need for restoration of power, we need to understand where we came from as God's New Covenant people. In this lesson we will move more rapidly through church history, in order to understand how far western church thought has strayed from the Biblical understanding of the supernaturally empowered church, and how it has occurred.

KEY INSIGHTS

Disaster: 6th and 7th Century the roman empire is overrun and western civilization begins to crumble. The Roman empire collapses.

Decline:

- Cities emptied
- Education collapses
- Disease, depression and despair characterize life – emphasis moves from this life to the next life

Distortion: Jerome's translation of the Scriptures into Latin, the language of the people:

In James 5:16 "heal" is mistranslated as "save". Interestingly, the Greek verb "áomai" which Jerome mistranslated into the Latin for "save" in James 5:16, he accurately translated into the Latin for "heal" in Luke 5:17 and Luke 9:11.

> **James 5:16a**
>
> Therefore confess your sins to each other and pray for each other so that you may be healed... (NIV)
>
> **Luke 5:17**
>
> One day as he was teaching, Pharisees and teachers of the law, who had come from every village of Galilee and from Judea and Jerusalem, were sitting there. And the power of the Lord was present for him to heal the sick. (NIV)
>
> **Luke 9:11**
>
> but the crowds learned about it and followed him. He welcomed them and spoke to them about the kingdom of God, and healed those who needed healing. (NIV)

Anointing to heal became Extreme Unction to prepare for dying.

Desert Divines: The decline in morality of leaders in the church leads those in search of the purity and power of earlier days to move to the desert of North Africa.

- These monastic movements were holiness revival movements within the Church.
- These Desert Fathers operated in healing.

- Eventually it was thought that only these desert divines were holy enough to move in healing power. "Normal" persons who did were suspected of operating by the power of the Devil.

Arabs, Aristotle and Aquinas (1200-1517 A.D.)

- Arabs conquer much of the former Christian lands in the areas of North Africa, Turkey and Southern Spain

- Aristotle's philosophy becomes the basis for the rising Arab culture

- Aquinas attempts an Apology appropriate for the Arabs

- There results an Aquinas-Aristotelian synthesis

Yet at the end of his life Aquinas had changed. St. Thomas Aquinas, Dec. 6th 1273: "I can write no more. All I have written seems so much straw compared with what I have seen and what has been revealed to me."

Three months later he died on a mission trip for the Pope. Others had to finish his famous Suma Theologica; we do not know how his experience would have changed his theology had he lived long enough to process the experience into his theology.

Scholasticism, Skepticism, Scofield and Sanctification (1517-1900 A.D.)

Scholasticism:

On Oct. 30th 1517, the 95 Theses were nailed to the door of Whittenburg Church, marking the beginning of the Protestant Reformation. The Reformers never challenged the Aquinas-Aristotelian Synthesis. In search of authority, the Reformers became more anti-supernatural, more opposed to healing than Roman Catholicism. In reaction to the accusation of the Roman Catholic Church's claim to the miraculous still in its midst as a basis of authority, the Protestants became cessationist, attributing the miracles in the Catholic Church to being false miracles or of the devil. The Roman Catholic Church was perceived to be the Great Whore of Revelation and the Pope the Antichrist.

The Reformers did not understand that power flows out of relationship, not doctrine!

Skepticism:

The Scientific Revolution on the continent of Europe produced skepticism in the church. Germany and England were profoundly affected. The anti-supernatural view of Higher Criticism spread, eventually reaching the shores of the United States. In Roman Catholicism Gifts of the Spirit as understood by Pope Gregory the Great, were:

- Wisdom
- Science
- Understanding
- Counsel
- Fortitude
- Piety
- Fear

Pope Gregory X: "No longer can the Church say, "Silver and Gold, have I none." Thomas Aquinas: "Yes, but neither can it any longer say, 'Rise and Walk.'"

Skepticism:

American Cyrus I. Scofield was heavily influenced by dispensationalist John Nelson Darby. Scofield had a dispensational view of the history and cessationist view of the end times. He believed that God's dealings with man were broken up into 7 periods of time or dispensations. In this system, the miraculous ceased with the apostles. His views were widely propagated and gained major influence in the notes of the Scofield Bible.

Ironically, the closed dispensational system of interpretation that Scofield propagated may have violated its own standard. Dispensationalists did not believe in the revelation and addition of "new" doctrine by esoteric experiences such as visions and dreams. Yet some have documented that key elements of the eschatological system of interpretation he adopted from Darby can be traced back to the visions of a young Scottish invalid named Margaret MacDonald.[1]

The Holiness issue in the 19th century opens the door to healing ministry: "Faith Cure" movement:

1. These revival movements centered on a desire for holiness and a desire for a return to Apostolic Christianity.

2. There were two main branches:

   - Those of Methodist (Armenian) roots believed it took years of struggle to experience.

   - Those of Baptistic (Calvinist) roots entered into holiness quickly by Faith. This branch was centered in England with Keswick and spread from there. This understanding translated over to receiving healing by Faith.

Endnotes

[1] *From Chapter 10, "Boiling It Down": "We have seen that a young Scottish lassie named Margaret MacDonald had a private revelation in Port Glasgow, Scotland, in the early part of 1830 that a select group of Christians would be caught up to meet Christ in the air before the days of Antichrist. An eye-and-ear witness, Robert Norton M.D., preserved her handwritten account of her pre-trib rapture revelation in two of his books, and said it was the first time anyone ever split the second coming into two distinct parts, or stages. His writings, along with much other Catholic Apostolic Church literature, have been hidden many decades from the mainstream of evangelical thought and only recently resurfaced. Margaret's views were well-known to those who visited her home, among them John Darby of the Brethren. Within a few months her distinctive prophetic outlook was mirrored in the September, 1830, issue of The Morning Watch and the early Brethren assembly at Plymouth, England. " MacPherson, Dave, The Incredible Cover-up (Medford, OR.: Omega Publications, 1999), p. 93*

NOTES

CHAPTER 8

CHARISMATA THROUGH HISTORY 3

LESSON GOALS

1. In this lesson we finish our walk through Christian history examining the historical continuation of the Charismata.
2. In this lesson we will seek to understand the developments in the period up to 1900 – Present: Pentecostalism, Persecution, Princeton, Prophecy and Power 1900-2004.

INTRODUCTION

In this lesson we survey what has happened in the church since the twentieth century.

KEY INSIGHTS

Pentecostalism, Persecution, Princeton, Prophecy and Power (1900 A.D.-Present)

Pentecostalism: Preparation for Pentecost

1. The Holiness Movement

2. Holiness Movement's connection to healing: Faith Cure Movement

    a. A. J. Gordon, pastor of Clarendon Street Baptist Church in Boston

    b. A. B. Simpson, Founder of Christian Missionary Alliance

    c. Andrew Murray from South Africa Dutch Reformed Church

Persecution

1. George Campbell Morgan, "Pentecostalism is the last vomit of Satan"

Personal Illustration: I have preached in his pulpit, teaching a series on healing at the request of his successor, R.T. Kendall, who succeeded D. Martyn Lloyd-Jones (1899-1981).

2. Phineas Bresee, President of the newly formed Nazarene Church

Princeton Theological Seminary

1. B. B. Warfield, "Counterfeit Miracles"

As we saw in detail in Parts 1-3 of this series Princeton Theological Seminary was the last bastion of Reformed Calvinistic cessationist teaching in the fight against the threat of Liberalism on the one hand and of the threat (real or perceived) of the establishment of religious authority through the operation of miracles. Warfield polemic still echoes today, hence our purpose for this series.

2. Hank Hannagraaf's "Counterfeit Revival" same presuppositions, same arguments.

Sometimes I have heard Hank make reference to some of the famous Healers within the Pentecostal/Charismatic tradition as being influenced by Gnosticism, an early heresy of the church. He does this by mentioning that Gnostics believed they had special understanding and revelation of the Scriptures. Hank states that the Gnostics created a new understanding of Jesus, which was not the true Jesus.

I agree Gnosticism was a serious heresy. However, I raise the question about the influence of Gnosticism upon Protestantism.

Gnosticism

- The Gnostics thought matter was evil and the spirit was good.

- They denied the reality of Jesus' incarnation, and any need for a literal resurrection.

- They placed no value upon the "flesh" here used for our corporal bodies. Because of this they did not believe in healing.

- Irenaeus was writing to refute Gnosticism, and his is the most impressive list of kinds of healings to be seen in the church, said explicitly that Christians were not practicing deception on people. The followers of Gnosticism, for whom he was writing, simply did not believe such things were possible.

An influence of Gnosticism is the devaluing of the natural body, the flesh, and an overvaluing of the spirit. In this scheme the value of healing of the flesh is totally lost; the ministry of our Lord's compassion has no place in Gnosticism.

Which Jesus?

In answer to the oft asked question of "The Bible Answer Man", "Which Jesus are the faith healers preaching?" Let me answer:

- If the Jesus we preach today has not the power to heal the sick, it is not the Jesus of the Gospels.

- If His Body on the earth today does not have the power to heal the sick, then it is still in the "dark ages" of the life of the Church. It does not represent the Lord, and the Body of Christ is not reflecting a connection with the Head, Jesus Christ.

- If we preach a Jesus who is not concerned about our physical bodies today, then it is a Jesus with a Gnostic influence and a departure from historic Judeo-Christian heritage.

The Cross: The Atonement and the Victor!

Hank is also concerned about the understanding of the Cross or the atonement on the part of certain ministers of healing. He is concerned that they are departing from the historic understanding of the cross. He is especially concerned about references to Jesus descent into hell. However, Church history indicates that this was accepted as "orthodox" teaching for hundreds of years within Christianity.

Furthermore, the understanding of the Cross from a "Substitutionary Atonement" viewpoint is not the only accepted understanding of the Cross.

- The major understanding of the Cross for the first 600 years of Christianity was "Christ is Victor". "Gustav Aulen has shown conclusively, up to the seventh century the atonement was seen by nearly all the church fathers in terms of victory over just such actual spiritual beings of some sort."[1]

- But, how are we to understand the theological backdrop to this view of the cross, the atonement? It is rooted in an understanding of evil and how Christ's death brought victory to those who had been affected by the "fall" and "evil's effect".

"It was believed that man's disobedience in Adam resulted in "death," which was more than simple physical dissolution of the body. In this first falling away an alien and de-

structive spirit entered men's lives, which gained power over them, corrupting both body and soul.... Its power was expressed in man's life spiritually by sin and mental illness, and physically in bodily disease which led eventually to physical death. Illness was not in fact the will of God, but directly and antagonistically opposed to it. Then on Golgotha Christ met the forces of "death," submitted to them and conquered them. Through his cross and resurrection the power of "death" (the Evil One) was defeated, so that by following his Way men could find rescue from both (italics his) sin and sickness. The early church knew these forces which Christ defeated. They had dominated mankind up to that time and still ruled most men. They were described in the New Testament, particularly by Paul, as "dominions," "thrones," "principalities," "spiritual wickedness," "the dragon," "death," and a variety of colorful names."[2]

Healing Follows from Jesus the Victorious One

Naturally the early church sought out the sick to care for them and heal them, just as it sought out sinners and tried to convert them. Healing was rescuing men from the domination of the enemy. This was the natural function of Christians as members of the body of Christ.

It was not by chance that Christian churches came to be regarded as healing shrines of Aesculapius. It was also natural that in many places the Christian churches should take over the function of those temples as the pagan religion died out.

In confrontation with the pagan world, the uniqueness of Christianity was clear. Celsus, who warned second-century pagans about the dangers of the new religion, sneered at Christians because sick and sinful people were acceptable to their God, who would not cast them off, and who indeed had sent his son to serve them.

Almost two centuries later the emperor Julian the Apostate gave much same picture of fourth century pagans and Christians when he wrote: "These impious Galileans give themselves to this kind of humanity: as men allure children with a cake, so they . . . bring converts to their impiety . . . . Now we can see what makes Christians such powerful enemies of our gods. It is the brotherly love which they manifest toward strangers and toward the sick and the poor."[3]

Prophecy

1. Branham and Angel in cave near Jeffersonville, Indiana 1946

2. Sharon Orphanage, 1947 (They had been to a Branham meeting, and had been reading "Fasting God's Secret to Atomic Power" William Hall) – Focused on the Spirits operation restore among the people.

3. Healing Revival 1948 – Focused on "God's Man of Power."

4. Billy Graham 1949 – The Spirit moves among Evangelicals.

Power

1. The Secular City: Dr. Harvey Cox Harvard Divinity School
2. Fire from Heaven: Dr. Harvey Cox. "I was wrong!"
3. The Christianization of the Roman Empire by Dr. Ramsey MacMillan
4. Edward Miller in Argentina - Cry For Me Argentina - Latter Rain
5. Tommy Hicks in Buenos Aires, Argentina: Opened the country to Protestantism – Latter Rain
6. Dennis Balcome: China 1988, 60,000,000 believers, 1994 all over China – Latter Rain
7. Pastor Rene Terra Nov: Largest Church in Manaus, Brazil - formerly Baptist – now over 48,000 members, just 10 years ago had 700 members.
8. Largest Baptist Church in Brazil: 30,000 members LaGoinia Baptist Church in Belo Horizonte
9. Videira Church in Goiania, Brazil: 7-8,000 in less than 10 years. In October 2003, they had a goal to Baptize 3,000 in one service in the public square. They did it!
10. Leif Hetland: Pakistan
11. Heidi Baker: Mozambique
12. Reinhard Bonnke: Africa

Endnotes

[1]*Morton T. Kelsey, Healing and Christianity (New York, NY: Harper and Row, Publishers, 1973, 1976 (paperback)) p. 145*

[2]*Ibid. p. 144*

[3]*Ibid. p. 147*

NOTES

CHAPTER 9

DELIVERANCE: A NEW TESTAMENT REALITY

LESSON GOALS

1. To gain a Biblical understanding of the spiritual world as it relates to the origin, nature and hierarchy of Satan and the demonic host, their operation and relationship to sickness.

2. To understand how Jesus dealt with the demonic host.

INTRODUCTION

This lesson is designed to give a basic Scriptural foundation regarding the demonic, in preparation for entering into deliverance (or liberation) ministry guided by the Pablo Bottari model of ministry.

KEY INSIGHTS

The Origin of Demons

There are three views regarding the origin of demons:

- They are disembodied human spirits from an earlier age.

- Demons are the offspring of the union between the sons of God and the daughters of men (Genesis 6:1-4).
- The view I hold and the one historically held by the Church is that they are the fallen angels.

The Order or Government of Demons

Demons appear to be the lowest among the ranks of the beings of evil

There are several passages where the Apostle Paul lists what appears to be a hierarchy within the realm of dark evil beings. There are two passages in Colossians. The first refers to their defeat by Christ on the cross:

> **Colossians 2:15**
>
> And having disarmed the powers and authorities, he made a public spectacle of them, triumphing over them by the cross.

In this second passage, Paul lists even more of the order of government of heavenly beings from which the evil beings fell with Satan (see below):

> **Colossians 1:16**
>
> For by him all things were created: things in heaven and on earth, visible and invisible, whether thrones or powers or rulers or authorities; all things were created by him and for him.

In Ephesians, Paul further describes division and qualifies these beings of evil:

> **Ephesians 6:12**
>
> For our struggle is not against flesh and blood, but against the rulers, against the authorities, against the powers of this dark world and against the spiritual forces of evil in the heavenly realms.

These beings came into being with Satan's fall. These thrones, powers, rulers, authorities of evil were not established by God, however. God is not the author of evil. They came into being by the fall of Lucifer and the third of the heavenly court that followed him in his rebellion against God.

> **Luke 10:17-18**
>
> The seventy-two returned with joy and said, "Lord, even the demons submit to us in your name." He replied, "I saw Satan fall like lightning from heaven.

> **Revelation 12:7-9**
>
> And there was war in heaven. Michael and his angels fought against the dragon, and the dragon and his angels fought back. But he was not strong enough, and they lost their place in heaven. The great dragon was hurled down—that ancient serpent called the devil, or Satan, who leads the whole world astray. He was hurled to the earth, and his angels with him.

Physical Illness and Demons

Not all illness or disease is caused by demons. The understanding that all sickness was caused by demons was a common view of many "Healing Evangelists", but it doesn't seem to be the biblical picture – the Bible clearly delineates between people who are physically or mentally sick from those who are demonized. Counting the repetitions, there are about 80 references to demons in the New Testament. Of these 80 there are 11 references which indicate a clear distinction between illness caused by demons and illness caused by other factors.

Let's look at a few of these passages:

> **Matthew 4:24**
>
> News about him spread all over Syria, and people brought to him all who were ill with various diseases, those suffering severe pain, the demon-possessed, those having seizures, and the paralyzed, and he healed them.

> **Matthew 8:16**
>
> When evening came, many who were demon-possessed were brought to him, and he drove out the spirits with a word and healed all the sick: various diseases, those suffering severe pain, the demon-possessed, those having seizures, and the paralyzed, and he healed them.

> **Matthew 10:8**
>
> Heal the sick, raise the dead, cleanse those who have leprosy, drive out demons. Freely you have received, freely give.

Mark 1:32-34

That evening after sunset the people brought to Jesus all the sick and demon-possessed. The whole town gathered at the door, and Jesus healed many who had various diseases. He also drove out many demons, but he would not let the demons speak because they knew who he was.

Mark 6:13

They drove out many demons and anointed many sick people with oil and healed them.

Mark 16:17-18

And these signs will accompany those who believe: In my name they will drive out demons; they will speak in new tongues; they will pick up snakes with their hands; and when they drink deadly poison, it will not hurt them at all; they will place their hands on sick people, and they will get well.

Luke 4:40-41

When the sun was setting, the people brought to Jesus all who had various kinds of sickness, and laying his hands on each one, he healed them. Moreover, demons came out of many people, shouting, "You are the Son of God!" But he rebuked them and would not allow them to speak, because they knew he was the Christ.

Luke 9:1-2

When Jesus had called the Twelve together, he gave them power and authority to drive out all demons and to cure diseases, and he sent them out to preach the kingdom of God and to heal the sick.

Luke 13:32

He replied, "Go tell that fox, 'I will drive out demons and heal people today and tomorrow, and on the third day I will reach my goal.'"

Acts 19:11-12

God did extraordinary miracles through Paul, so that even handkerchiefs and aprons that had touched him were taken to the sick, and their illnesses were cured and the evil spirits left them.

The results of demonization are not exclusively mental or nervous. Here is a specific example of a demonized mute man being healed by the casting out of a demon:

> **Matthew 9:32-33**
>
> While they were going out, a man who was demon-possessed and could not talk was brought to Jesus. And when the demon was driven out, the man who had been mute spoke. The crowd was amazed and said, "Nothing like this has ever been seen in Israel."

The biblical examples are distinctly and peculiarly mental in two instances only.

- Gadarene maniac and parallel passages (Mark 5:1-20; Matthew 8:28-9:1):

> **Luke 8:26-39**
>
> They sailed to the region of the Gerasenes, which is across the lake from Galilee. When Jesus stepped ashore, he was met by a demon-possessed man from the town. For a long time this man had not worn clothes or lived in a house, but had lived in the tombs. When he saw Jesus, he cried out and fell at his feet, shouting at the top of his voice, "What do you want with me, Jesus, Son of the Most High God? I beg you, don't torture me!" For Jesus had commanded the evil spirit to come out of the man. Many times it had seized him, and though he was chained hand and foot and kept under guard, he had broken his chains and had been driven by the demon into solitary places. Jesus asked him, "What is your name?" "Legion," he replied, because many demons had gone into him. And they begged him repeatedly not to order them to go into the Abyss. A large herd of pigs was feeding there on the hillside. The demons begged Jesus to let them go into them, and he gave them permission. When the demons came out of the man, they went into the pigs, and the herd rushed down the steep bank into the lake and was drowned. When those tending the pigs saw what had happened, they ran off and reported this in the town and countryside, and the people went out to see what had happened. When they came to Jesus, they found the man from whom the demons had gone out, sitting at Jesus' feet, dressed and in his right mind; and they were afraid. Those who had seen it told the people how the demon-possessed man had been cured. Then all the people of the region of the Gerasenes asked Jesus to leave them, because they were overcome with fear. So he got into the boat and left. The man from whom the demons had gone out begged to go with him, but Jesus sent him away, saying, "Return home and tell how much God has done for you." So the man went away and told all over town how much Jesus had done for him.

- The demonized man who attacked the Jewish exorcists.

> **Acts 19:13-16**
>
> Some Jews who went around driving out evil spirits tried to invoke the name of the Lord Jesus over those who were demon-possessed. They would say, "In the name of Jesus, whom Paul preaches, I command you to come out." Seven sons of Sceva, a Jewish chief priest, were doing this. One day the evil spirit answered them, "Jesus I know, and I know about Paul, but who are you?" Then the man who had the evil spirit jumped on them and overpowered them all. He gave them such a beating that they ran out of the house naked and bleeding.

There is a distinction made between the demonized and the epileptic (also translated "lunatic" or "moonstruck" in some translations):

> **Matthew 4:24**
>
> News about him spread all over Syria, and people brought to him all who were ill with various diseases, those suffering severe pain, the demon-possessed, those having seizures, and the paralyzed, and he healed them.

Epilepsy is specified in one case only.

> **Matthew 17:15, 18**
>
> "Lord, have mercy on my son," he said. "He has seizures and is suffering greatly. He often falls into the fire or into the water… Jesus rebuked the demon, and it came out of the boy, and he was healed from that moment.

Children Can Become Demonized

Most people in America don't believe children can become demonized. We must remember that the forces of evil do not play by the rules of the Geneva Convention. There are no civilians in this war for souls, and women and children are special targets. I have been surprised to see small children demonized. Twice in the Bible we see children who are demonized, the Syro-Phonecian woman's daughter and the man's son who Jesus' disciples couldn't deliver.

Mark 7:25-26

In fact, as soon as she heard about him, a woman whose little daughter was possessed by an evil spirit came and fell at his feet. The woman was a Greek, born in Syrian Phoenicia. She begged Jesus to drive the demon out of her daughter.

Mark 9:14-29

When they came to the other disciples, they saw a large crowd around them and the teachers of the law arguing with them. As soon as all the people saw Jesus, they were overwhelmed with wonder and ran to greet him. "What are you arguing with them about?" He asked. A man in the crowd answered, "Teacher, I brought you my son, who is possessed by a spirit that has robbed him of speech. Whenever it seizes him, it throws him to the ground. He foams at the mouth, gnashes his teeth and becomes rigid. I asked your disciples to drive out the spirit, but they could not." "O unbelieving generation," Jesus replied, "how long shall I stay with you? How long shall I put up with you? Bring the boy to me." So they brought him. When the spirit saw Jesus, it immediately threw the boy into a convulsion. He fell to the ground and rolled around, foaming at the mouth. Jesus asked the boy's father, "How long has he been like this?" "From childhood," he answered. "It has often thrown him into fire or water to kill him. But if you can do anything, take pity on us and help us." "'If you can'?" said Jesus. "Everything is possible for him who believes." Immediately the boy's father exclaimed, "I do believe; help me overcome my unbelief!" When Jesus saw that a crowd was running to the scene, he rebuked the evil spirit. "You deaf and mute spirit," he said, "I command you, come out of him and never enter him again." The spirit shrieked, convulsed him violently and came out. The boy looked so much like a corpse that many said, "He's dead." But Jesus took him by the hand and lifted him to his feet, and he stood up. After Jesus had gone indoors, his disciples asked him privately, "Why couldn't we drive it out?" He replied, "This kind can come out only by prayer."

Note the texts refer to the girl as a little daughter and the man's father says the boy had been demonized from "childhood".

How Jesus Dealt with the Demonic

> **Mark 1:21-28**
>
> They went to Capernaum, and when the Sabbath came, Jesus went into the synagogue and began to teach. The people were amazed at his teaching, because he taught them as one who had authority, not as the teachers of the law. Just then a man in their synagogue who was possessed by an evil spirit cried out, "What do you want with us, Jesus of Nazareth? Have you come to destroy us? I know who you are—the Holy One of God!" "Be quiet!" said Jesus sternly. "Come out of him!" The evil spirit shook the man violently and came out of him with a shriek. The people were all so amazed that they asked each other, "What is this? A new teaching—and with authority! He even gives orders to evil spirits and they obey him." News about him spread quickly over the whole region of Galilee.

Jesus is never seen wrestling with someone to get their demons out. We never see Jesus wrestling or struggling with demon powers. He acted from a position of authority (vs. 27), manifesting the Father's kingdom:

> **Luke 11:20**
>
> But if I drive out demons by the finger of God, then the kingdom of God has come to you.

Jesus simply commands them to come out using the authority He had from the Father. He exercised kingdom authority and power through simple commands, which the demons had to obey:

> **Luke 4:36**
>
> All the people were amazed and said to each other, "What is this teaching? With authority and power he gives orders to evil spirits and they come out!"

Randy's Testimony: Sovereign Deliverance by Jesus Christ

My own personal deliverance was a sovereign deliverance. No one had to say anything to me, not one person said, "Come out!" The power of God completed the deliverance even when no one was sure I was having a deliverance.

This is where I hope to see the Church come to, but most of us do not walk in this level of power. That means we have to do deliverance with more emphasis on interviewing to determine the root causes and then leading them to forgive someone, ask forgiveness for their own sins, renounce vows and commitments of an ungodly nature and command the spirit to leave.

We will cover this in more detail in the upcoming lesson on the Argentine deliverance model.

The Ultimate End of Demons

The Bible makes some very clear statements concerning the ultimate end of Satan and the demonic host. Jesus said that the eternal fire had been prepared for the "devil and his angels". Again, these angels which fell with the Devil from heaven are the demons on the earth today. The Apostle John connects the destiny of the fallen angels with the destiny of the devil:

> **Revelation 12:7-9**
>
> And there was war in heaven. Michael and his angels fought against the dragon, and the dragon and his angels fought back. But he was not strong enough, and they lost their place in heaven. The great dragon was hurled down - that ancient serpent called the devil, or Satan, who leads the whole world astray. He was hurled to the earth, and his angels with him.
>
> **Matthew 25:41**
>
> Then He will say to those on His left, "Depart from me, you who are cursed, into the eternal fire prepared for the devil and his angels…"
>
> **Revelation 20:10**
>
> And the devil, who deceived them, was thrown into the lake of burning sulfur, where the beast and the false prophet had been thrown. They will be tormented day and night for ever and ever.

NOTES

CHAPTER 10

THE BASICS OF DELIVERANCE

Dr. Mike

LESSON GOALS

1. To understand how and where demonic attachment takes place
2. To understand how to remove demonic attachment
3. How to create a strong spiritual foundation and prevent further demonic attachment

INTRODUCTION

Scripture tells us not to give the devil a foothold. In this chapter, we'll be discussing how demonic attachment takes places, likely places attachments may take root and how to remove attachments.

KEY INSIGHTS

All attachments are not equal. Demonic influences in a life have varying levels.

Mark 5: 1-5

And they came to the other side of the sea, into the country of the Gerasenes. And when He had come out of the boat, immediately a man from the tombs with an unclean spirit met Him, and he had his dwelling among the tombs. And no one was able to bind him anymore, even with a chain; because he had often been bound with shackles and chains, and the chains had been torn apart by him, and the shackles broken in pieces, and no one was strong enough to subdue him. And constantly night and day, among the tombs and in the mountains, he was crying out and gashing himself with stones.

Mark 8:31-33

And He began to teach them that the Son of Man must suffer many things and be rejected by the elders and the chief priests and the scribes, and be killed, and after three days rise again. And He was stating the matter plainly. And Peter took Him aside and began to rebuke Him. But turning around and seeing His disciples, He rebuked Peter, and said, "Get behind Me, Satan; for you are not setting your mind on God's interests, but man's."

Luke 9:38-40

And behold, a man from the multitude shouted out, saying, "Teacher, I beg You to look at my son, for he is my only boy, and behold, a spirit seizes him, and he suddenly screams, and it throws him into a convulsion with foaming at the mouth, and as it mauls him, it scarcely leaves him. "And I begged Your disciples to cast it out, and they could not."

Luke 11:14

Jesus was driving out a demon that was mute. When the demon left, the man who had been mute spoke, and the crowd was amazed.

Matthew 12:22

Then they brought him a demon-possessed man who was blind and mute, and Jesus healed him, so that he could both talk and see.

Luke 13:11

A woman was there who had been crippled by a spirit for eighteen years. She was bent over and could not straighten up at all.

Where does a demon attach itself to a person?

Body/Soul/Spirit

> **1 Thessalonians 5:23**
>
> "Now may the God of peace Himself sanctify you entirely; and may your spirit and soul and body be preserved complete, without blame at the coming of our Lord Jesus Christ."

We are body, soul and spirit. Our spirit is where we connect with God. We are created as spirit beings. Sin separates us from God and we are cut off from God. Our spirit still functions but it was designed to connect and relate to God. When we ask Christ to come into our lives, God's Spirit connects with our spirit as we are joined with Jesus. God's Spirit bears witness with our spirit that we are children of God (Rom. 8:16). Our soul is also part of our inner man. It is our mind (our capacity to think), our will (our capacity to choose) and our emotions (our capacity to feel). Our bodies are the temple of the Holy Spirit. Our bodies give us our physical identity and enable us to relate to the physical world.

At salvation we were totally redeemed, body, soul and spirit. The spirit was fully redeemed as God's Spirit connects with our spirit. Our soul (our mind, will and emotions) has also been redeemed. 1 Cor 2:16 says that you have the mind of Christ. Your will has been redeemed. Phil. 2:13 says that God is in you to will and to work for His good pleasure. God gives you the desire and the power to do His will. Your emotions have also been redeemed. He has given you the fruit of the Holy Spirit of love, joy, peace, patience, kindness, gentleness and so on. What has been redeemed must be reclaimed. Since God's Spirit indwells your Spirit, I believe it has been fully reclaimed. The soul must now be reclaimed.

The body is under the curse of death, but 1 Cor. 15 tells us that it will be full reclaimed.

"Opportunity" - opportunity, power, place of operation, an area of legal control. In a kingdom it is the right of jurisdiction over land determined by the authority of the king.

> **2 Corinthians 4:16**
>
> "Therefore we do not lose heart, but though our outer man is decaying, yet our inner man is being renewed day by day."
>
> **Ephesians 4:26-27**
>
> In your anger do not sin. Do not let the sun go down while you are still angry, and do not give the devil an opportunity.

NIV - Don't give the devil a "foothold."

KJV - Don't give the Devil a 'place'.

NRSV - Do not make "room" for the devil.

NCV - Do not give the devil a way to defeat you.

Demons Look for a "Right" (a "Place") to Attach

Our demonic adversary wants to destroy our life. He wants us to self-destruct. The demonic look for a legal "right" to attach themselves to a person. If we grant such permission and give him such an "opportunity" or "foothold" in our lives through our sin, someone else's sin or any open door that they think gives a legal entrance. These become inroads into our life that if left unresolved will eventually bring us to a place where we eventually become enslaved. At the point of enslavement, we call it a "stronghold". Even after we have given our lives to Jesus, the demonic will try to stay if we have given ground over to the kingdom of darkness. These attachments may come by our choice, by our neglect or by their deception. They must be seen as illegal squatters that have no right to the believer and must be evicted. We must reinforce what Jesus bought and paid for on the cross. Remember that the devil doesn't play by fair rules. He cheats. He is a liar, a thief and a murderer. If he thinks he has a right, he will claim it. He is a legalist and looks for loopholes. He seizes what he can.

Some common "opportunities" that open doors to the demonic (not an exhaustive list):

- habitual sin
- sexual perversion and pornography
- involvement in occult practices
- cult involvement, voluntary and involuntary
- drugs
- ancestral or generational sin
- curses
- trauma
- involuntary exposure to evil
- unforgiveness
- wounding of the heart

How to Remove Demonic Attachments

Handwritten notes: Habitual Sin, Trauma, Unforgiveness (Bitter root judgement), Generational curses

- Remove their right to be there. Heal the hurt - fix the crack and they slide *off*

- Reinforcing the work of the cross. Often there is no legitimate right that remains. The shed blood of the cross destroyed the works of the devil and removed the curse of the law. The demons are just trespassers that need to be evicted and you are not only serving them their eviction notice, but you are removing them immediately from the premises. That is within your jurisdiction to enforce.

Don't Leave the "House" Empty. Fill the "House" through Rebuilding a Godly Stronghold in the Opposite Spirit

Whenever you tear down an ungodly demonic stronghold, you rebuild that area with a Godly stronghold. You want to fill the house! It's for your protection!

> **Matthew 12:43-45**
>
> When an evil spirit leaves a person, it goes into the desert, seeking rest but finding none. Then it says, 'I will return to the person I came from.' So it returns and finds its former home empty, swept, and clean. Then the spirit finds seven other spirits more evil than itself, and they all enter the person and live there. And so that person is worse off than before. That will be the experience of this evil generation.

Ungodly Stronghold	Godly Stronghold
Pride/Self-Promotion	Humility
Self-Hate	Self-Acceptance/Love
Rejection	Acceptance
Lust/Greed	Contentment
Hate	Love
Fear	Trust
Depression	Joy

Anxiety...Peace

Rudeness..Kindness

Bitterness..Compassion

Rage..Self Control

Rebellion...Submission

This is not an exhaustive list, nor is everything necessarily demonic.

NOTES

NOTES

CHAPTER 11

DELIVERANCE: A TEN-STEP MINISTRY MODEL

LESSON GOALS

1. To understand the Pablo Bottari Ten-Step deliverance model, to be a peaceful and loving participate in the ministry of deliverance (liberation).

INTRODUCTION

> **Matthew 4:24**
>
> So his fame spread throughout all Syria, and they brought him all the sick, those afflicted with various diseases and pains, those oppressed by demons, epileptics, and paralytics, and he healed them. (ESV)
>
> **Mark 16:17**
>
> And these signs will accompany those who believe: in my name they will cast out demons; they will speak in new tongues; (ESV)

In this session we will take what we have already learned about the New Testament reality of deliverance and build on it by discussing specifics for moving in deliverance ministry. We want to emphasize that "seeing a demon under every bush" or behind every problem is not

Biblical. Then again, neither is the denial of their existence or operation. Sadly, many who could be helped, especially in Western societies, are denied assistance because of the lack of practical instruction or by theologies which deny their need. It is not unusual to read accounts of western missionaries who have quickly changed their theology when confronted openly with demonic activity of the field in Asia, Africa and South America.

To review, deliverance is setting a person free from the oppression of a demonic spirit.

Note: the term "oppression" is used here, rather than "possession", because "possession" implies ownership and complete control. Since a believer has been purchased by the Lord Jesus Christ he cannot be "possessed" by Satan or his emissaries. However, many believers have been host to demonic presences in their years before conversion, and these evil spirits do not always cease operation against them when their host is converted.

For years, Pablo Bottari supervised the deliverance tent at evangelist Carlos Anacondia's crusades in Argentina. There he supervised deliverance ministry to many thousands, and personally participated in the deliverance of many hundreds of people, mostly believers. He felt that the deliverance ministry he saw at first was noisy, difficult, lengthy and often humiliating to the person being ministered to.

He developed a ten-step model for deliverance which is quietly effective. The model discussed in this session is based on his. It is quiet, pastoral, loving, non-humiliating and very effective. It is followed in all Global Awakening crusades, conferences, international trips and in many churches

KEY INSIGHTS

The Pablo Bottari Deliverance Model

Presuppositions:

- We're ministering to the person, not the demon.
- Authority, not wrestling, is the focus.
- Counseling, bringing the truth, is key; quietness is better than flamboyant demonstrations of warfare.
- It is extremely important to find out the entry points, the "open doors" and how to close those doors.
- They don't have to "throw up" or be torn or tormented to be delivered. Satan loves to make a scene. We want to rob him of that opportunity.

The Model's Ten Steps:

The following ten steps are followed in a session where the minister does not know the host person well, such as in a crusade or other public meeting setting. In some settings, some of these steps might be omitted. For example, where the minister knows the prayee is a believer and really wants to be set free, steps 4 and 5 would be omitted. If there is no manifestation during the ministry, step 2 and probably step 3 would be omitted. Remember: These steps are a model, a guide. Pray for the guidance of the Holy Spirit at all times!

1. Give the individual priority.

   a. Keep a loving attitude, not a militant attitude.

   Firmness is necessary in casting out a demon, but in the meantime, the prayee needs to feel loved and accepted.

   b. Be encouraging. Raise hope. Emphasize to the prayee that Jesus can bring them freedom.

   c. Don't emphasize the power of the demon; it is subject to you in the name of Jesus.

   Remember that the prayee may have been in bondage for years, and perhaps has received many prayers that were not completely effective.

2. If a spirit manifests, bring it under submission, in the Name of Jesus.

   a. Take authority over the spirit.

   Tell it, "Submit, in the name of Jesus!", or "Be quiet, in Jesus' name!" or similar commands. It is best to let the prayee know that you are not speaking to them, but to the demon.

   b. Repeat such commands until the spirit is quiet. [handwritten: get the prayee to tell it to stop! Don't be intimidated]

   c. Don't be surprised if this takes time. Be persistent.

   You may have to command the spirit several times – or even many times --to submit. It will come under submission.

   d. If others gather while you are quieting the spirit, ask them not to touch the prayee, and not to speak or pray loudly.

   Your objective is not to keep the spirit stirred up, but to <u>get the spirit to be quiet</u> so that you can <u>talk to the prayee.</u>

> **Mark 16:17**
>
> And these signs will accompany those who believe: in my name they will cast out demons; they will speak in new tongues; (ESV)

3. Establish and maintain communication with the prayee.

   a. You must be able to talk with the person receiving ministry, because you must have his cooperation if the deliverance is to be successful.

   b. If you are not sure the prayee can hear you, ask - even if the person's eyes are closed.

   c. Maintaining communication may require additional commands to the spirit to submit, during ministry.

   The prayee may drop his head, close his eyes, or let his eyes may wander. Ask him to hold his head up, to open his eyes, to look at you. If the person cannot do these things, a spirit is involved and you should order the spirit to submit.

4. Ask the prayee what s/he wants to be free from, and try to make sure s/he really wants to get free.

   a. In a crusade situation, ask the person receiving ministry what he wants to be freed from.

   If the prayee is uncertain, ask them what the speaker was praying about when the spirit started to manifest.

   Other helpful initial questions are whether he is trying to break any habit without success, or whether he has any conduct he considers odd or unusual.

   b. In private ministry, the prayee probably will know what the bondages are that he or she wants to be set free from.

   This can include one or two specific bondages, or it may involve a broader ministry – a thorough housecleaning. The prayee may have communicated this information in advance to the person who will be ministering.

   c. If the prayee indicates that he does not want ministry even though a spirit has manifested, abide by that decision.

   d. If the prayee wants to leave after partial ministry, allow the person to leave.

   You may encounter attitudes that indicate lack of desire for complete freedom.

   e. Do not try to detain the prayee or to minister against his or her will.

5. Make sure the prayee <u>understands to make Jesus Christ Lord and Savior.</u>

   a. The ministry recipient will need the help of the Holy Spirit to stay free.

   If he is not a Christian, he probably will be back in bondage shortly, even if he is delivered. This should be explained to him. It isn't wise to try to deliver him in the hope that he will become a believer as a result of getting free.

   > **Matthew 12:43-45a**
   >
   > When an evil spirit comes out of a man, it goes through arid places seeking rest and does not find it. Then it says, 'I will return to the house I left.' When it arrives, it finds the house unoccupied, swept clean and put in order. Then it goes and takes with it seven other spirits more wicked than itself, and they go in and live there. And the final condition of that man is worse than the first..."

   b. If you can lead the person to Christ, do. <u>If you can't, pray for him; bless him.</u>

   <u>Pray for the healing of his hurts and wounds.</u> Let him know by your attitude that you are not offended. Be loving, but don't cast out any spirits. Explain why you won't, because he won't be able to stay free. Encourage him to take the step of making Jesus his Lord and Savior and then return for deliverance.

6. Interview the prayee to discover the event or events, <u>the conduct or the relationship situations</u> that have led to his or her bondage or bondages.

   a. The purpose is to expose where forgiveness is required and where healing, repentance and breaking of bondages are needed.

   b. <u>Find all open doors.</u> If there is no obvious place to start, begin with his parental relationships, then move to other areas. Be thorough, don't rush.

   c. Do not stir up demons, keep them quiet. List the spirits encountered and areas requiring (forgiveness of others or repentance). *Lust/porn.*   *have them Renounce*

   d. <u>Consider breaking a curse</u> if the person has persistent difficulty in an area of life.

   e. <u>Fear is an entry point</u> for many different spirits (and a problem in many illnesses).
   (II Tim - not given a spirit of fear - TRUST)

7. Lead the prayee in <u>"closing" these "doors"</u> to the admission of spirits.   *Father, I forgive them / You forgive them / I release them*

   a. <u>Forgive whoever caused the hurt</u> or led him into wrong conduct.

   b. <u>Repent and ask forgiveness for specific sins.</u>

   It is important to be specific, such as, "Father, forgive me for ____ (hate, bitterness, sharing my body with ____, reading horoscopes, etc.)."

c. Renounce all sins or spirits involved in the name of Jesus.

- Renunciation should be audible and firm.

- Renunciation is not a prayer to God. It is spoken to the spirit involved, who is an enemy. It should be spoken as a command to an enemy, not a petition to God.

- Spirits taken in without the sin of the prayee need to be renounced the same as those that entered through his wrong attitudes or other fault. For example, if a child witnesses his parents fighting (verbally or physically), he may take in spirits of confusion, anxiety, fear, insecurity and others.

- Renounce all spirits involved, in the name of Jesus. In the case of sex outside marriage, the person should renounce spirits taken in from every partner he can recall, individually, by first names if possible.

- Pacts with Satan and inner vows must be renounced and curses broken, such as "In the name of Jesus I renounce the spirits of _____ and _____" or "In the name of Jesus, I renounce the vow I made never/always to _____."

d. *The minister should break the yoke of bondage and the power of any spirit.*

This closes the door. You or the seeker can do this:

- "In the name of Jesus I break the power of the spirit(s) of _____ over (person's name) so that when they are cast out, they will not come back."

- "In the name of Jesus I break the power of every curse over (person's name) from _____(father's careless critical words, mother's rejection, etc.)."

8. When all doors are closed, cast out the unclean spirit or spirits.

    With all doors closed, the spirits will leave quickly and quietly.

    If they don't leave promptly, go back to Step 6. Tell the person there may be other spirits to deal with. Re-interview. Ask the Holy Spirit to show you or the seeker or a team member what He wants to do next.

9. Lead the prayee in a prayer of praise and thanksgiving to Jesus for his or her deliverance.

    If the person cannot speak, or if spirits manifest, more doors need to be closed.

10. Have the prayee ask the Holy Spirit to fill him/her, to fill up every space formally occupied by an evil spirit.

    We don't want to leave the house swept clean and empty! Spend time praying for an infilling of the Holy Spirit! You want them to leave in love with Jesus and rejoicing in His strength, power, and love!

Post Ministry Suggestions:

1. Walking in forgiveness as a lifestyle.

- Explain that forgiveness is a decision, not a feeling, and that he can forgive a person even if he doesn't feel like it. He can choose to forgive. His spirit can have the rule over his emotions, and it is important to forgive for his own best interest.

- The prayee needs to know that the forgiveness process – of needing to forgive the same person more than once (sometimes many times) – is normal and not a sign that the deliverance ministry was a failure.

2. Asking the Lord for healing quickly after being hurt.

3. Instruct them to commit to accountability, such as in an accountability/cell home group in the person's local fellowship.

4. Suggesting ways to change crucial habit patterns. Some possibilities are:

- Praise God, singing or listening to praise songs, reading Psalms.
- Pray in tongues.
- Take authority over tempting spirits in the name of Jesus and send them away.
- Thank God for having been set free. This is very important!
- If he falls, he can repent quickly and get the door closed again.
- If Satan accuses him of being a sinner, he can say: "You're right, Satan. Just look at what Jesus has forgiven me for!"
- He can look for ways to remind himself that Jesus is his Lord. You can tell him that a number one priority should be to make Jesus the Lord over every area of his life.
- Ask daily for infilling of the Holy Spirit.

5. Taking authority over any spirits that may try to attack or torment him or her again in the future.

6. Praying in tongues.

7. Daily Bible reading, having intimate quiet time with God.

8. Things that the Holy Spirit may prompt concerning walking in the light.

The following chart can be used as a guideline for common things to be "tuned in" for as you minister:

Body	Soul			Spirit
Sexual sin of any kind	Resentment/ Anger	Despair/ Hopelessness	Despair/ Hopelessness	Any occult experience
Uninvited sexual relationship	Trauma and its effects	Pride/ Arrogance	Criticism/ Gossip	Witchcraft/ Manipulation
Long Illness/ General Weakness	Rejection/ Loneliness	Rebellion/ Vengeance	Envy in all forms	Satanism/ Freemasonry
All Addictions	Unforgiveness/ Bitterness	Fear in all forms	Greed	Curses/ Inner vows

NOTES

NOTES

CHAPTER 12

GROWING IN CONFIDENCE

LESSON GOALS

1. To clarify your identity and power as a child of the King.

INTRODUCTION

One of the biggest roadblocks I see in Christians seeking to walk in healing is a lack of confidence. In this lesson, we will be discussing the scriptural basis for understanding and walking in your authority in Jesus.

KEY INSIGHTS

What God Calls You to He will Empower

> **Matthew 4:23**
>
> Jesus traveled throughout Galilee teaching in the synagogues, preaching everywhere the Good News about the Kingdom. And He healed people who had every kind of sickness and disease.

When Jesus taught His disciples to advance the Kingdom of God, He modeled and taught them to do two things... DECLARE the Kingdom and DEMONSTRATE the Kingdom. The demonstration gave opportunity to declare the Kingdom or demonstrated validated the declaration. A part of that demonstration was the casting out of demons.

> **Luke 9:1-2**
>
> And He called the twelve together, and gave them power and authority over all the demons, and to heal diseases. And He sent them out to proclaim the kingdom of God, and to perform healing.
>
> **Luke 10: 1,9**
>
> Now after this the Lord appointed seventy others, and sent them two and tow ahead of Him to every city and place where He Himself was going to come...and heal those in it who are sick, and say to them, 'The kingdom of God has come near to you.'
>
> **John 14:12**
>
> "Truly, truly, I say to you, he who believes in Me, the works that I do shall he do also; and greater works than these shall he do; because I go to the Father.
>
> **1 Corinthians 2**
>
> And when I came to you, brethren, I did not come with superiority of speech or of wisdom, proclaiming to you the testimony of God. For I determined to know nothing among you except Jesus Christ, and Him crucified. And I was with you in weakness and in fear and in much trembling. And my message and my preaching were not in persuasive words of wisdom, but in demonstration of the Spirit and of power, that your faith should not rest on the wisdom of men, but on the power of God.

Live Convinced of the Completed Work of Jesus

You must live convinced of the absolute victory of Jesus over the Kingdom of Darkness. You have to be convinced that Jesus has absolute authority in heaven and on earth.

> **Romans 8:38-39**
>
> For I am convinced that neither death nor life, neither angels nor demons, neither the present nor the future, nor any powers, neither height nor depth, nor anything else in all creation, will be able to separate us from the love of God that is in Christ Jesus our Lord.

> **Matthew 28:18**
>
> Jesus came and told his disciples, "I have been given complete authority in heaven and on earth.
>
> **Ephesians 1:21-22**
>
> Now he (Jesus) is far above any ruler or authority or power or leader or anything else in this world or in the world to come. And God has put all things under the authority of Christ, and he gave him this authority for the benefit of the church.

You have to be convinced that the Devil has been completely stripped of all authority.

Dwell on the Greatness of God

> **Colossians 2:15**
>
> God stripped the spiritual rulers and powers of their authority. With the cross, he won the victory and showed the world that they were powerless.

Secure in your Authority in Jesus

You and Jesus are ONE – (principle of unification).

> **2 Kings 6:15-18**
>
> Now when the attendant of the man of God had risen early and gone out, behold, an army with horses and chariots was circling the city. And his servant said to him, "Alas, my master! What shall we do?" So he answered, "Do not fear, for those who are with us are more than those who are with them." Then Elisha prayed and said, "O LORD, I pray, open his eyes that he may see." And the LORD opened the servant's eyes, and he saw; and behold, the mountain was full of horses and chariots of fire all around Elisha.

- I died with Christ
- I was buried with Christ

1 John 5:13

I write this to you who believe in the Son of God, so that you may know you have eternal life.

2 Corinthians 5:17

Therefore if any man is in Christ, he is a new creature; the old things passed away; behold, new things have come.

- I was raised with Christ

Ephesians 2:6

For He raised us from the dead along with Christ, and we are seated with Him in the heavenly realms--all because we are one with Christ Jesus.

- I am seated with Christ

    You need to know that you have the right to walk out and exercise that authority.

Ephesians 1

I pray that the eyes of your heart may be enlightened, so that you may know what is the hope of His calling, what are the riches of the glory of His inheritance in the saints, and what is the surpassing greatness of His power toward us who believe. These are in accordance with the working of the strength of His might which He brought about in Christ, when He raised Him from the dead, and seated Him at His right hand in the heavenly places, far above all rule and authority and power and dominion, and every name that is named, not only in this age, but also in the one to come. And He put all things in subjection under His feet, and gave Him as head over all things to the church, which is His body, the fullness of Him who fills all in all.

1 John 2:6

Whoever claims to live in Him must walk as Jesus did.

> **Luke 10:18-20**
>
> And He said to them, "I was watching Satan fall from heaven like lightning. Behold, I have given you authority to tread upon serpents and scorpions, and over all the power of the enemy, and nothing shall injure you. Nevertheless do not rejoice in this, that the spirits are subject to you, but rejoice that your names are recorded in heaven."

Identity Statement for Ministering Deliverance

I am a child of the King. I am a co-heir with Jesus.

All Jesus bought and paid for is my inheritance.

I am united with Jesus. I have been crucified with Christ.

I died with Him. I was buried with Him. I was raised with Him.

I am seated with Him in the heavenlies far above all rule, all power, all authority,

and above every name that is named, not only in this age, but also in the one to come.

Therefore I carry the authority of Christ.

I have authority over sickness, over sin, over the flesh, over demons, and over the world.

I am the salt of the earth. I am the light of the world.

I will displace the darkness. I have the full armor of God.

I put on the breastplate of righteousness, the belt of truth, the helmet of salvation,

the sandals of peace. I take up the shield of faith, and the sword of the Spirit,

for the weapons of my warfare are not fleshly.

They are divinely powerful to tear down the strongholds of darkness.

I can do all things through Christ, because greater is He who is in me

than he who is in the world.

NOTES

CHAPTER 13

BREAKING FREE: PART 1

LESSON GOALS

1. To understand the gift of spiritual discernment and to learn to recognize the difference between natural and demonic mental and physical afflictions.

2. What questions to ask and what to be aware of during a deliverance.

3. How to rebuke a demon and command it to go.

INTRODUCTION

With deliverance, you will need to recognize that when you are dealing with the demon. Even so, you must always give priority to the person. The act of deliverance should be an act of love, freeing the person. It's about the person and their freedom.

KEY INSIGHTS

How do you know you are dealing with a demon?

Through Spiritual Discernment

The gift of discerning of spirits discerns if the spirit operating is the Holy Spirit, a demonic spirit or the human spirit. You need to be aware of any spiritual "caution flags" that go off inside of you that God will use to help you discern.

Remember that not everything is demonic. If someone is mentally ill, that doesn't mean they are demonized. The brain is an organ and can malfunction like a liver, a heart colon, etc. The unfortunate thing is that some people want to put every mental malfunction in the category of being demonized. The malfunction of the brain may be a physical issue, a spiritual issue or both. It might be caused by a demon or have a demon present, but you can't assume that every brain or mental dysfunction is demonic. You need to listen to the Holy Spirit.

If a person went through abuse when they were really young, they may have developed patterns of disassociation where the brain went into survival mode and their brain partitioned so that some parts of their brain disassociated with other parts. It was a protective pattern that enabled them to survive as children, but becomes dysfunctional as adults if it still remains. They end up going through life with a mind that is fragmented, with fragmented personalities and memories. The brain is wonderfully made. The body is designed to survive. But these disassociated parts aren't demons. There may be demons attached to some and maybe there are some demons masquerading as a disassociated personality, but the healing of that person isn't through casting out a bunch of demons, but through the healing of the inner wounds.

Through Observing Certain Physical Manifestations

This could be things like:

- The pain in the body is moving around
- Sudden drowsiness, possibly even a drunken stupor
- Facial contortions
- Screaming
- Rigid body
- Eye rolling around, a lack of eye contact
- Changing voices
- ...a whole lot more

A physical manifestation doesn't mean that there is a demon present, but should be investigated. Demons don't always manifest, but don't be surprised when they do.

Through Asking Probing Questions:

- Do they hear voices?
- Do they have uncontrollable sin?

- Do they possess habitual uncontrollable behavior?
- Are they ruled by abnormal emotions?
- Are they ruled by self-hatred?

The person you are dealing with must ALWAYS be given priority. You must see them as an important person that God loves. You must give them honor as God's creature. They may have some significant emotional hurts that may have opened the door to the demonic. The deliverance should be an act of love. Since our priority is the healing of the person, we don't sacrifice the person by laying them on the altar of an agenda of deliverance that would scar and wound the person in the process. When people feel loved, deliverance goes faster.

Rebuke the demon and tell it to go

Just tell the unclean spirit to go. Don't always presume the demon has a "right"; their "right" is usually not legitimate. They may be loosely attached. I only go down the road of looking for legal rights if they don't leave after a moment or two of telling the unclean spirit to leave.

Involve Their Will

In rebuking the demons, include the person to be a participant. There is great power in their will. There is power in agreement. Often that demon is present because the person came into agreement with something. This agreement empowers the demon. The solution requires the person to come into agreement with the will of God and to get this unclean spirit out. It is best to teach them how to fight. If you don't, you might find yourself fighting their battles for them.

If the demon doesn't leave after a moment or two, we have to investigate "WHY" it still remains.

When they don't go, there are a couple of reasons why. Here we need to investigate if there is still a "right" that this demon is still attached to. Is there a door that needs to be shut? Is there a foothold that needs to be taken back?

- Has the reason why this demon was attached in the first place been thoroughly removed?
- Is there no desire or intent to "occupy" the land?

Matthew 12:43-45

"When an evil spirit leaves a person, it goes into the desert, seeking rest but finding none. Then it says, 'I will return to the person I came from.' So it returns and finds its former home empty, swept, and clean. Then the spirit finds seven other spirits more evil than itself, and they all enter the person and live there. And so that person is worse off than before. That will be the experience of this evil generation."

Exodus 23:29-30

But I will not do this all in one year because the land would become a wilderness, and the wild animals would become too many to control. I will drive them out a little at a time until your population has increased enough to fill the land.

Close the "right" or "open door" given to the demon, then remove the demon

Once you establish that there is still a right or an open door in which a demonic spirit is still attached to, then give attention to that area and remove its right. Break the agreement. Once the "right" is removed, then command the spirit to submit and go.

CHAPTER 14

BREAKING FREE: PART 2

LESSON GOALS

1. To learn about the power of words, the creation of curses and soul ties, how to break free of them, and how to renounce previous involvement in the occult.

INTRODUCTION

The words we speak have more power than we realize. In this lesson, we will discuss curses and soul ties, how they come about and how to break free of them. We will also discuss declarations and using them to free ourselves and others.

KEY INSIGHTS

Breaking the Power of Words that Bring a Curse

> **Genesis 11:1,6**
>
> Now the whole earth used the same language and the same words... And the LORD said, "Behold, they are one people, and they all have the same language. And this is what they began to do, and now nothing which they purpose to do will be impossible for them."

1 Corinthians 1:10

Now I urge you, brothers, in the name of our Lord Jesus Christ, that you all say the same thing, that there be no divisions among you and that you be united with the same understanding and the same conviction.

John 17:21-23

My prayer for all of them is that they will be one, just as you and I are one, Father--that just as you are in me and I am in you, so they will be in us, and the world will believe you sent me. "I have given them the glory you gave me, so that they may be one, as we are-- I in them and you in me, all being perfected into one. Then the world will know that you sent me and will understand that you love them as much as you love me."

Matthew 12:36-37

And I say to you, that every careless word that men shall speak, they shall render account for it in the day of judgment. "For by your words you shall be justified, and by your words you shall be condemned."

What you send out of your mouth will come back to you.

Luke 6

But I say to you who hear, love your enemies, do good to those who hate you, bless those who curse you, pray for those who mistreat you. But love your enemies, and do good, and lend, expecting nothing in return; and your reward will be great, and you will be sons of the Most High; for He Himself is kind to ungrateful and evil men. Be merciful, just as your Father is merciful. And do not judge and you will not be judged; and do not condemn, and you will not be condemned; pardon, and you will be pardoned. Give, and it will be given to you; good measure, pressed down, shaken together, running over, they will pour into your lap. For by your standard of measure it will be measured to you in return.

It is your birthright to be free from the bondage of the curse of words.

> **Galatians 3:13**
>
> Christ redeemed us from the curse of the Law, having become a curse for us - for it is written, curse is everyone who hangs on a tree.
>
> **Ephesians 4:29**
>
> Let no unwholesome word proceed from your mouth, but only such a word as is good for edification according to the need of the moment, that it may give grace to those who hear.

Prayer

In the name of Jesus,

I break every curse of words against me.

I take every word captive that has been spoken over me,

...that I spoke over myself.

And I break the power those curses from hell.

I cancel every assignment of darkness.

I cast them to the ground.

I call blessing to fall on me in their place.

I take back every curse I have spoken against another.

I cast those words down to the ground.

I return a blessing on those with whom I have cursed.

Jesus took my cursing so I can live in blessing.

Renounce Previous or Current Involvement in any Occult or Cultic Practices

> **John 14:5-6**
>
> Jesus said to him, "I am the way, and the truth, and the life; no one comes to the Father, but through Me."

Prayer

In the name of Jesus,

I renounce any involvement in (name the occult or the cultic practice).

I renounce (list the practices you participated in).

I ask you God to forgive me for worshipping other Gods.

I declare that Jesus is the way, the truth, and the life.

No one comes to the Father but through Him.

Jesus is Lord of all, I will worship God and Him alone.

Genesis 2:23-24

And the man said, "This is now bone of my bones, And flesh of my flesh; She shall be called Woman, Because she was taken out of Man." For this cause a man shall leave his father and his mother, and shall cleave to his wife; and they shall become one flesh.

Matthew 19:5-6

And said, 'For this cause a man shall leave his father and mother and shall cleave to his wife; and the two shall become one flesh'? Consequently they are no longer two, but one flesh. What therefore God has joined together, let no man separate. (see also Mark 10:8-9 & Ephesians 5:31 which also quote the Genesis 2 text)

1 Corinthians 6:16

Or do you not know that the one who joins himself to a harlot is one body with her? For He says, "The two will become one flesh."

1 Corinthians 6:18

Run away from sexual sin! No other sin so clearly affects the body as this one does. For sexual immorality is a sin against your own body.

Psalms 23:3a

He restores my soul...

> **1 Thessalonians 5:23**
>
> Now may the God of peace Himself sanctify you entirely; and may your spirit and soul and body be preserved complete, without blame at the coming of our Lord Jesus Christ.

Breaking Soul Ties

Since restoration of the soul is the intention of the Lord, then there must be a way to bring restoration of the soul that has been fragmented in unholy soulish relationships. Based on the intention of God for soul restoration and the dilemma of soul fragmentation by unholy sexual unions, we deduce that God grants permission and authority to call our souls into holy alignment. We can confidently ask the Lord to restore our souls into wholeness. We can ask the Lord to restore what we have lost or have given away that rightfully belongs to us and to send away what isn't ours to keep.

Prayer

In the authority of Jesus,

I plead the Blood of Jesus

To stand between me and _____(this person)_____,

And separate the "one flesh" union.

I send back to them everything that I have taken from them

...when I became "one flesh" with him/her.

I call back to me

...everything that I gave in this "one flesh" union.

I declare the blood of Jesus to be a wall of separation between us.

Thank You Jesus for restoring my soul.

Breaking the Generational Curses

> **Number 14:18**
>
> The LORD is slow to anger and abundant in lovingkindness, forgiving iniquity and transgression; but He will by no means clear the guilty, visiting the iniquity of the fathers on the children to the third and the fourth generations.
>
> **Isaiah 28**
>
> So listen to the Lord's message, you who brag, you leaders in Jerusalem. You say, "We have made an agreement with death; we have a contract with death. When terrible punishment passes by, it won't hurt us. Our lies will keep us safe, and our tricks will hide us." Because of these things, this is what the Lord GOD says: "I will put a stone in the ground in Jerusalem, a tested stone. Everything will be built on this important and precious rock (cornerstone). Anyone who trusts in it will never be disappointed. I will use justice as a measuring line and goodness as the standard. The lies you hide behind will be destroyed as if by hail. They will be washed away as if in a flood. Your agreement with death will be erased; your contract with death will not help you. When terrible punishment comes, you will be crushed by it.
>
> **Numbers 6:24-27**
>
> The LORD bless you and keep you, the LORD make his face shine upon you and be gracious to you; the LORD turn his face toward you and give you peace."' "So they will put my name on the Israelites, and I will bless them."

Prayer

In the name of Jesus,

I declare the blood of Jesus to stand between me and the _____ generation as a wall of separation.

I cancel every assignment of darkness and remove every right of the demonic to afflict me because of the sin of that generation. I call to me my righteous inheritance and the blessings of that generation.

Forgive and Release

What forgiveness is and what it is not:

- Forgiveness IS acknowledging an offense.

- Forgiveness is NOT saying this didn't happen to you.
- Forgiveness is NOT saying what they had done was OK.
- Forgiveness IS forgiving a debt.
- Forgiveness IS giving up any unrealistic or unfulfilled expectations.
- Forgiveness is NOT reconciliation.
- Forgiveness is NOT releasing the proper boundaries that could prevent future damage.
- Forgiveness IS releasing you to get on with life to fulfill your destiny.

> **Romans 12:19**
>
> Never take your own revenge, beloved, but leave room for the wrath of God, for it is written, "Vengeance is Mine, I will repay," says the Lord.

Unforgiveness has consequences?

- The tormentors are unleashed against those who refuse to forgive. (Matthew 18:21-35)
- You curse yourself. (James 3:8-10, Luke 6:38, Matthew 12:37)
- Possible, and very likely, physical problems
- You can cut off the impartation of the blessings that another can give you.
- Your offender still has power over you until you forgive.

Forgiveness IS releasing the offender into the care of Jesus, the Just Judge, who is your defender.

Prayer

In the name of Jesus,

I choose to forgive as I have been forgiven.

I now choose to forgive _____.

I release any right I have retained ...to bring revenge.

I release them from my hands,

And place them into Your hands, my Just Judge.

I break every curse I have sent to them.

I call forth a blessing towards them.

Removing the Slime from a Fear Bond

I will live in perfect love that casts out fear.

I cast off the yoke of domination.

I now choose to forgive _____ (name the person).

I break the power of their words over me.

I break the victim spirit off of me.

I rebuke the fear of man I have lived under.

I cancel my bond to them.

I take back my true identity.

I will not live under oppression.

I receive my Father's love.

I am now free to live and to love.

Final Thoughts

- Cover yourselves and family members with the blood of Jesus. Put on the full armor of God.
- Work as a team.
- Depend on the word of knowledge and discerning of spirit gifts.
- The Holy Spirit is the deliverer.
- Teach them how to fight or you will always fight their battles for them. Their will MUST be involved.
- Be relaxed and don't shout and don't wrestle the people. Yelling doesn't increase your authority.
- A manifesting demon is the last thing they want to do.
- Be aware of those whose assignment is to drain you of energy and distract.

- Take extra care in dealing with children.
- Don't pursue demons.
- Not everything is demonic.
- Don't listen to their threats - they lie.
- Angels are present.
- Deliverance is Jesus' ministry, not yours. Jesus delivers. You just get to watch and speak when you are told.

Take Time to Deslime

After ministering to the demonized, take time to dust off any residue from that encounter. Ask the Lord to wash everything off of you, to cancel any assignments of hell, and release the assignments of heaven over you and your team. Ask Him to keep you minds pure, to guard your emotions, to protect your body, and bless those you who would curse you.

Affirmation Declaration

There is only one true and living God, ...who exists as the Father, Son, and Holy Spirit Jesus Christ is the Christ, the only way to the Father.

Jesus destroyed the works of the devil.

He disarmed the rulers and authorities,

...having triumphed over them

...through His shed blood on the cross.

Jesus now has all authority in heaven and on earth.

Jesus has authority over sin, He has authority over sickness He has authority over death, He has authority over the world, He has authority over the devil.

He has redeemed me from hell and has given me a new destiny.

I am saved by grace through faith and not of my works.

Jesus delivered me from the domain of darkness and transferred me to His kingdom.

I have been forgiven of all my sin.

I am now ONE with Jesus.

I died with Christ. I was buried with Christ,

I rose with Christ. I am seated with Jesus in the heavenlies.

Because I am one with Jesus,

I am righteous, I am holy, I am a saint.

I will live above sin because I am prone to do righteousness.

I am not prone to sin any more.

I am a new creature, the old is gone.

The new has come.

Because of my oneness of Jesus,

I have authority over sin, over the world, over the devil.

I can resist the devil and he will flee form me.

God has given me spiritual weapons, and spiritual armor.

I can live a victorious life.

I can do all things through Christ.

I will overcome in this world.

Because greater is He who is in me,

Than he who is in the world.

CHAPTER 15

CESSATIONISM

LESSON GOALS

1. Introduce the topic of Cessationism and understand the relevance today of evaluating B.B. Warfield's *Counterfeit Miracles*.

2. Define Cessationism and its key tenets.

3. Review a brief history of Cessationism's development in Church history.

4. Understand the stage of development of cessationism as *defined in Calvinism*.

LESSON GLOSSARY

apologist: one who speaks or writes in defense of someone or something

glossolalia: speaking in tongues

hermeneutics: the study of the methodological principles of interpretation (as of the Bible)

polemic: an aggressive attack on or refutation of the opinions or principles of another
presupposition: a conditional element in logic or fact

INTRODUCTION

> **Matthew 9:35**
>
> Jesus went through all the towns and villages, teaching in their synagogues, preaching the good news of the kingdom and healing every disease and sickness.
>
> **Matthew 10:7-8**
>
> As you go, preach this message: 'The kingdom of heaven is near.' Heal the sick, raise the dead, cleanse those who have leprosy, drive out demons. Freely you have received, freely give.
>
> **1 Corinthians 4:20**
>
> For the kingdom of God is not a matter of talk but of power.
>
> **1 Thessalonians 1:5a**
>
> Because our gospel came to you not only in word, but also in power and in the Holy Spirit and with full conviction.
>
> **Matthew 24:14**
>
> And this gospel of the kingdom will be preached in the whole world as a testimony to all nations, and then the end will come.

To begin, let us look at a quote from Jon Ruthven in his book *On the Cessation of the Charismata: The Protestant Polemic on Postbiblical Miracles*:

> *Historically, Pentecostalism has provoked controversy at almost every stage of its development. This has been true not merely because of its tradition-breaking forms of worship and practice, but, significantly for the purposes of this essay, because the emergence of Pentecostalism was a tangible challenge to a theological position maintained in the church for centuries: that the miraculous gifts of the Holy Spirit had ceased. Against this, the salient characteristic of Pentecostalism is its belief in the present-day manifestation of spiritual gifts, such as miraculous healing, prophecy and, most distinctively, glossolalia. Pentecostals affirmed that these spiritual gifts (charismata) are granted by the Holy Spirit and are normative in contemporary church life and ministry*[1]

As described in Vinson Synan's book, In the Latter Days, the Pentecostal fire that broke out at the beginning of the 20th century and spread literally around the world is indeed a formidable "tangible challenge" to the cessasionist position that the miraculous charismata have ceased. During the 1960s and 1970s it set ablaze believers within mainline Protestantism and Roman Catholicism in the Neo-Pentecostal/Charismatic renewal. In the 1980s its flames ignited Evangelicalism and other mainline groups in the Third Wave movement. Synan describes this last development's effects:

> The coming together of evangelicals and charismatics in the 1980s presaged other changes in American church life. Although little had been said by mission boards of the mainline churches, Pentecostalism had long since swept into the mission fields of other denominations. Southern Baptists whispered the rumor that an estimated 75 percent of their missionaries had spoken in tongues in the various "renovation" and charismatic movements in the third world during the 1970s. Large numbers of Methodists, Presbyterians, Anglicans, and Lutheran missionaries had become practicing Pentecostals on the field – a fact they did not broadcast back home.
>
> The latter rain was also falling in the major independent seminaries of the nation as well as in many of the denominational schools. This led to a fever of research and writing on the doctoral level on all things pertaining to Pentecostalism.
>
> A sign of the times in the academic world was the development of the most popular course ever offered at Fuller Theological Seminary. Taught by professors John Wimber and Peter Wagner, "Signs, Wonders and Church Growth" attracted some 100 students to study the use of the gifts of the Spirit in the churches. Wimber's classes often ended with prayer for the sick, tongues, and prophecies. Wimber put his theories into practice in his "Vineyard Christian Fellowship" congregation in Yorba Linda, California, where 4000 persons attended Sunday worship services in a church that by 1982 was only five years old.
>
> As large numbers of young converts from the "Jesus movement" felt the call to preach, they increasingly entered seminaries and schools of theology to prepare for the ministry. By 1983, about one third of the student bodies of Fuller and Gordon Conwell seminaries were made up of Pentecostals or charismatics. Many of these graduates were called to serve traditional mainline congregations as pastors, musicians, and ministers of Christian education. By the 1980s they were being welcomed with open arms and with few questions asked about their charismatic experiences.[2]

According to Synan, "While few mainline theologians would accept the Pentecostal theory of initial evidence, there was a tendency after 1970 to accept the premise that the gifts of the Spirit were operative in modern times, and to reject the old theory of the cessation of the charismata."[3] Yet, according to Ruthven the growth of the Pentecostal-charismatic movement "did not occur without opposition"[4]:

> The cessationist polemic, which was often directed against persons or groups claiming religious authority via any exhibition of divine healings, prophecies or miracles, recurs consistently from within such conflict settings throughout the history of the church and even within rabbinic Judaism. But it emerged in its modern form most prominently in the conflict between Rome and the Protestant reformers, notably Calvin, then again during the

> *Enlightenment in '[sic] the 'great debate on miracles', and presently in the twentieth-century opposition to the Pentecostal-charismatic movement. In recent years the advancing front of charismatic growth has precipitated showers of polemical books and tracks, virtually all reiterating the cessationist premise.[5]*

In a footnote reference to the "showers of polemical books and tracks" Ruthven lists over 25 books and articles dealing with the "cessationist polemic" response to the Pentecostal/Charismatic/Third Wave movement.[6] Possibly one of the most well-known, highly available works listed - clearly a modern representative of the cessationist polemic - is *Charismatic Chaos* (Grand Rapids, MI: Zondervan, 1992) by John F. MacArthur, Jr. In his introduction, Dr. MacArthur acknowledges what Synan documents--the rapid spread of this "tangible challenge" to cessationism:

> *Through modern communication media – especially television – the charismatic movement has swept the globe and is expanding at a rapid pace. Charismatic teaching has now reached beyond the United States and Europe to the remotest parts of South America, the Orient, Africa, India, the South Pacific, Eastern Europe, and the Soviet Union – nearly everywhere the name of Christ is known. Literally millions worldwide believe God is giving people signs, wonders, and miracles on a scale unprecedented since Biblical times. These claims continue to multiply at a rate so prolific that they can hardly be cataloged, let alone verified.[7]*

MacArthur also expresses disconcert at its further spread to the "formerly wary" through their attraction to the Signs and Wonders movement and its "notion":

> *Some even go so far as to deny the effectiveness of evangelism without such miracles. They argue that the gospel message is weakened or nullified if not accompanied by great signs and wonders. They believe some people need to see signs and wonders before they will believe. That notion has spawned a whole new movement, grandiosely tagged "the Third Wave of the Holy Spirit," also known as the Signs and Wonders movement....This recent variation on the old charismatic theme is attracting many evangelicals and others from mainline denominations who were formerly wary of Pentecostal and charismatic influences.[8]*

Ruthven, introducing the purpose of his book's study, makes an interesting observation concerning the response to the cessationist polemic as represented by books such as MacArthur's *Charismatic Chaos*:

> *Many political and theological works either express directly or presuppose the position that the miraculous gifts of the Holy Spirit had ceased. In response, some defenders of present-day charismata established their case of historical studies which endeavor to show a more or less continuous line of charismatic activity throughout the centuries.*
>
> *Despite the relatively large size of the Pentecostal charismatic constituency, there has been – with a small, but growing, number of exceptions – little scholarly effort to trace and evaluate the cessationist position, including its historical and Biblical aspects, from a perspective of systematic theology.[9]*

In Ruthven's book - which is just such a scholarly response to the cessationist position - he explains his focus on analyzing the cessationist polemic writings of B.B. Warfield:

> *The doctrine that miraculous gifts of the Holy Spirit ceased around the apostolic age has evolved over the long expanse of church history, and has found expression in various religious persuasions and philosophical convictions. This study evaluates the historical levels of influence from John Calvin to Warfield and the rationale for this cessationist polemic. It focuses in particular upon B.B. Warfield's thought because this represents the historical culmination of the cessationist tradition and because Warfield was the most prominent modern evangelical advocate for the position. His thought is singled out here because he stands at or near the end of the evolution of cessationism, works within Calvinism, the dominant religious tradition espousing this position, and is steeped in the modern philosophical presuppositions which undergird the recent expressions of cessationism.*[10]

He further explains Warfield's immense theological influence even today:

> *To most theological leaders of millions of evangelicals and fundamentalists in North America, the collection of Warfield's work in The Inspiration and Authority of the Bible stands as the definitive statement on the nature of biblical revelation... He also produced a definitive statement for evangelicals on another issue: the occurrence of modern-day miracles. In the evangelical debates over the continuation of charismatic gifts, Warfield's Counterfeit Miracles remains, after seven decades, the major starting point for this discussion as well. Accordingly, this study treats Warfield's Counterfeit Miracles as the final, authoritative and representative expression of cessationism for conservative American evangelicalism.*[11]

Ruthven cites numerous sources to support his assessment of the centrality of Warfield's influence.[12]

It is our goal in this series of lessons entitled "B.B. Warfield, His Counterfeit Miracles, and Today's Echoes" - using Ruthven's analysis as a framework - to show the failure of the cessationist polemic of B.B. Warfield, and to validate what we believe to be the biblical understanding for the function and duration of the charismata.

KEY INSIGHTS

To avoid getting lost in the details, let's start out by getting a framework of the basic concepts and issues of this study and our plan of analysis.

Cessationism Defined

Cessationism is, simply stated, the doctrine that revelatory and miraculous charismata[13] passed away with the apostolic age. What is telling is the great inconsistency among cessationists as to what "passed away with the apostolic age" really means. Ruthven says of R.W. Graves, author of *Tongues Shall Cease: A Critical Survey of the Supposed Cessation of the Charismata*, Paraclete 17 (Fall 1983).

He notes in cessationist writings the bewildering and imprecise variety of points at which the charismata are believed to have ceased, for example, after the writing of 1 Corinthians, the book of Hebrews, or the last New Testament book; at the closing of the canon of Scripture; when the New Testament was 'accepted' or 'circulated'; at the death of the last apostle; the death of the last disciple on whom the apostles confirmed a charism; when the apostolic age passed; at the destruction of Jerusalem; when the Church matured in 'love' or in 'doctrine'; until faith was established; ' when the whole knowledge of God designed for the saving the health of the world had been incorporated into the living body of the world's thought'.[14]

Is it possible that this confusion is evidence of inconsistencies and contradictions intrinsic to the cessationist polemic? We believe so, and will later examine why.

Cessationism As Expressed in Warfield's Polemic

According to Ruthven, Warfield's polemic is an expression of the traditional, Protestant cessationist propositions of classic, post-Reformation Calvinism which can be summarized as follows:

The essential role of miraculous charismata is to accredit "normative" or "true" Christian doctrine and its bearers. While God may providentially act in unusual or striking ways, true miracles are limited to epochs of special divine revelation, i.e., those of the Biblical period Miracles are judged by the doctrines they purport to accredit. Therefore, if doctrines are false or alter orthodox doctrines, then the accompanying miracles are necessarily counterfeit.[15]

Warfield's Cessationism: Its Central Failure

In the Scripture verses at the beginning of this lesson the Gospel of the Kingdom - as proclaimed and demonstrated by Jesus Christ, his disciples and the apostle Paul - is presented to be one not just of words, but also of power. Warfield, a staunch defender of the miraculous (as he defines it) within the Biblical period, vehemently denies and discredits their operation in the post-biblical period. Why the contradiction? Where is the failure?

We strongly agree with Ruthven's assessment:

The central failure of Warfield's cessationism is the confusion of the sufficiency of revelation, that is, in the unique historical manifestation of Christ and apostolic doctrine as finally revealed in Scripture, with the procedural means of communicating, expressing and applying that revelation, that is, via the charismata, including gifts of prophecy and miracles. In other words, the charismata do not accredit the Gospel; they express the Gospel.[16]

A central goal in this study - through an analysis of Warfield's cessationist polemic - is to show just how untenable his position, and to demonstrate that the charismata are indeed a valid, continuing expression of the Gospel of the Kingdom for the present time.

Evaluating Warfield's Cessationist Polemic

In his book's introduction, Ruthven states:

> *Warfield's polemic—the culmination of a historically evolving argument directed against certain threats to institutional religion—fails because of internal inconsistencies with respect to its concept of miracle, its historical method and its biblical hermeneutics. Insofar as these errors are characteristic of more contemporary forms of cessationism, the latter also fail.*[17]

Ruthven describes Warfield's polemic as "the culmination of a historically evolving argument" directed against certain threats to institutional religion". He attributes its failure to internal inconsistencies with respect to its:

- Concept of miracle
- Historical method
- Biblical hermeneutics

A Brief History of Cessationism's Development

We now move on to look at a brief history of cessationism. As Ruthven notes:

> *Warfields's cessationism did not, of course, suddenly appear in its highly evolved form at the beginning of the twentieth century. Cessationism developed from a complex stew of post-biblical theologies and philosophies that had long been simmering in their polemical cauldron...Cessationism did not originate within orthodox Christianity but within normative Judaism and in Christian sects during the first three centuries of the Common Era.*[18]

We will begin our overview by examining the development of cessationism in Judaism and the early period of Christian History. This will be followed a look at cessationism's development in the Protestant Reformation and the Enlightenment.

Cessationism and Judaism

According to Ruthven, there emerged three major cessasionist elements within Judaism.[19] A developing ambivalence about prophecy and miracles in the "post-biblical (Old Testament) period:

> *...from the outset of the Maccabean Judaism harbored an ambivalence about prophecy and miracles: lamenting, on the one hand, the loss of prophets and God's miraculous interventions, and on the other, a readiness to accept reports of such activity when it appeared.*[20]

This led to a tendency to view prophecy and miracles on a two-tier level, the top tier being the classical prophets and miraculous events described in Scripture and the lower tier being the attenuated forms of prophecy and miracles, such as:

- *"bot qol"*, literally, "daughter of a voice," suggesting an inner voice or revelatory impression[21]

- Miracle accounts of early rabbis

As we shall discover, Warfield echoes a similar two-tier view when evaluating his "concept of miracle" in order to delineate what constitutes a "true" miracle in the biblical versus post-biblical periods. The view that the Spirit's activity had already peaked:

> ...the feeling nonetheless persisted that the highest level of the Spirit's activity had ended [Emphasis added], so that by the end of the first century CE, an unusually pious rabbi might 'merit' the Holy Spirit (that is, the gifts of prophecy and miracles), but not receive it because post-biblical (OT) generations are not worthy.[22]

Note three things:

- The quasi-cessation delineation between the biblical and post-biblical (Old Testament) periods.

- The idea of individual 'merit'—where the reception of gifts of prophecy and miracles accredited 'pious' individuals operating in those gifts.

- The implied overriding qualitative difference between the biblical and post-biblical periods, which, as we shall see, is similar to the "Golden Age" ideas prevalent in Enlightenment thinking.

The reaction of religious authorities to the charismatics:

> ...the issue of religious authority between charismatics who...may have wished to use prophecy and miracle to establish their doctrinal credibility, increasingly lost out to those who relied on the interpretive skill and consensus of the academy. Prophecy and miracle working were replaced by study of the Torah and its scholarly interpretations.[23]

According to Ruthven, Judaism reacted to two elements:

> Radical charismatic messianic pretenders revolting against Roman rule. The rapidly growing charismatic Christian movement. Judaism became a religion based on the one true God, the written Torah and its scholastic interpretation. Because of that miracles and prophecies, perforce, had ceased.[24]

As we shall observe, a similar pattern of cessationism developed within Christian History.

Cessationism in the Early Church

Ruthven documents a number of sources in the development of cessationist thinking in the first several centuries of Church history. We review these now to gain an understanding of the gradual early cessationist transition where "miracles and prophecy" are "replaced by piety and the study of Scripture."[25]

Early Christian Apologists

Early Christian apologists such as Justin (c. 100-c. 165), Origen (c. 185-c.254) and Cyril (315-386) used the Jewish admission that prophecy and miracles had ceased among them to argue that God had transferred them to the church as proof of God's favor. For example, Origin wrote:

> God's care of the Jew was transferred to those Gentiles who believe in him. Accordingly [they] have not even any vestige of divine power among them. They no longer have any prophets or wonders, though traces of these are to be found to a considerable extent among Christians. Indeed, some works are even greater; and if our word may be trusted, we also have seen them.' (Contra Celsum 2.8)[26]

Since the coming of Christ no prophets have arisen among the Jews, who have admittedly been abandoned by the Holy Spirit.[27] Ruthven explains:

> Thus the church moved toward evidentialism, the view that the primary, if not exclusive, function of miracles is to accredit and vindicate a doctrinal system or its bearers.

In reference to the following commentary by E. Sjöbert:

> At the beginning, however, the Gentiles too could receive the Holy Spirit, and there could thus be prophets among them. But after Balaam misused his prophetic gift, the Holy Spirit was taken from the Gentiles and reserved for Israel.[28]

Ruthven points that the very cessationist evidential argument the Jewish apologists had once argued was now used on them:

> This whole line of argument must have been ironically familiar to Jews who had often argued that at one time Gentiles had experienced the Holy Spirit, but...the Spirit was totally transferred from any Gentile participation to the Jews alone.[29]

A Montanist Prophetess (c. end of 2nd century)

Near the end of the second century with Montanism there arose a prophetess named Maximilla. She is alleged to have made the cessationist claim, "After me there will be no more prophecy, but the end[*]" probably referring to Jesus statement in Matthew 28:20b, "...I am with you always, to the very end[*] of the age." Ruthven explains:

> Against this hint of cessationism some appealed to 1 Cor. 13.10 ["but when the perfect comes, the partial will be done away." (NASB)]. For example Eusebius records that Miltiades does so against Maximilla and concludes: 'it is necessary that the prophetic charisma be in all the church until the final coming'.[30]

The irony here is that the verse used by Miltiades to counter Maximilla's [cessationist] claim is used by later cessationists to argue AGAINST the continuation of the charismata. According to Gordon Fee:

Others see "the perfect" as referring to the full revelation given in the NT itself, which when it would come to completion would do away with the "partial" forms of charismatic revelation. Given its classical exposition by B. B. Warfield, this view has been taken over in a variety of ways by contemporary Reformed and Dispensationalist theologies.[31]

*Greek "sunteleía," meaning "a point of time marking completion of a duration, completion, close, end."[32]

Victorian of Petau (d.c. 304)

In a commentary on the Apocalypse Victorian writes: "The apostles through signs, wonders and mighty deeds overcame the unbelievers. After this the faith of the Church was given the comfort of the interpreted prophetic Scriptures."[33] Ruthven comments that, "This seems to be the only clear connection between the cessation of the charismata and the replacement by Scripture among the church fathers."[34]

Chrysostom (347-407)

Chrysostom's "several dozen references to miracles are associated with arguments against seeking them"[35] which Ruthven summarizes as follows:

> *Miracles were once required for weak faith; Powerful miracles would perniciously allow weak faith among observers.*
>
> *When 'true religion took root' in all the world, miracles ceased.*
>
> *To suffer for Christ is much greater than to experience miracles delivering us from that suffering.*
>
> *No one should 'wait for miracles' today because the 'sign greater than all signs' is deliverance from sin.*
>
> *If we choose Christian love as the best spiritual gift, 'we shall have no need of signs.'*[36]

Isidore of Pelusium (d. c. 450)

Isidore "follows this latter line somewhat idealistically: 'Perhaps miracles would take place now, too, if the lives of the teachers rivaled the bearing of the apostles.'"[37]

Ambrosiaster (d. 384)

Ruthven describes how Abroisiaster taught a proto-cessationist theory of charismatic entropy, that is, the weakening in both frequency and level of power of the miraculous:[38]

- Level 1: Only the apostles (as promised in John 14:12) would perform 'greater works.'

- Level 2: John 20:22 denoted an impartation of the spirit for conferring ecclesiastical power which enabled the successive transfer of the spirit throughout history via the imposition of hands.

- Level 3: In Acts 2 the Spirit was bestowed on the laity 'whence arises the preaching of the church'.

Augustine (354-430)

Augustine began with strong cessationist sentiments:

> We have heard that our predecessors, at a stage of faith on the way from temporal things up to eternal things, followed visible miracles...When the Catholic Church had been founded and diffused throughout the whole world on the one hand miracles were not allowed to continue till our time, lest the mind should always seek things visible and the human race should grow cold by becoming accustomed to things, which, when they were novelties kindled its faith... At that time the problem was to get people to believe before anyone was fit to reason about divine and invisible things.[39]

Notice the weak faith /strong faith cessationist theme (similar to those expressed by Chrysostom):

> Weak, 'temporal' faith of the early church required the 'visible' miraculous 'novelties' 'to get people to believe.' is, to 'kindle' faith.

> Once the Church was established miracles 'were not allowed to continue' lest they undermine the maintenance of a mature faith 'fit to reason about divine and invisible things'.

> Yet near the end of his life Augustine in Chapter 22 of City of God repudiated his earlier position and provided accounts of over seventy miracles.[40]

One more point is in order. Another corollary argument of cessationism, of which Augustine is an example, is the "common tendency to transmute the 'miraculous' charismata of earlier times into the more 'ordinary' expressions of church ministry;"[41] Augustine wrote in *Sermons On the Selected Lessons of the New Testament*:

> The blind body does not now open its eyes by a miracle of the Lord, but the blinded heart opens its eyes to the world of the Lord. The physical corpse does not now rise again, but the soul rises again which lies dead in a living body. The deaf ears of the bodies are not now opened; but how many who have the ears of their hearts closed, let them fly open at the penetrating word of God.[42]

This argument gave "the ecclesiastical hierarchy with a ready rationale against complaints of diminished charismatic activity within their churches."[43]

Gregory the Great (540-604)

Gregory was "a prolific recorder of contemporary miracles" and "wrote (c. 590) what was to become a highly influential metaphor on the cessation of miracles."[44] To Gregory, at the Church's beginning miracles "...were necessary...for in order that faith might grow, it had to be nourished by miracles; for we, too, when we plant shrubs, pour water on them till we see that they have gotten a strong hold on the ground; and when once they are firmly rooted, we stop the watering. For this reason Paul says: 'tongues are for a sign, not to believers, but to unbelievers.'"[45]

Thomas Aquinas (1225-74)

Ruthven describes the centrality of Aquinas in cessationist thought:

> [Aquinas] ordered the pattern of cessationist tenets which dominated the church until the 20th century. His major new contribution to cessationism was the metaphysics of miracle based on Aristotelian philosophy. A true miracle, Aquinas said, expresses itself beyond any 'means' of nature, absolute and above the power of the created order: it must be purely 'super-natural'. Therefore, starting with the 'facts' of a miracle, an observer can reason to its divine source. While one can never know how God performed a miracle, one can certainly know that he did. Miracles, then, include such events as instantaneous healings of visibly diseased or broken bodies, the revelation through a prophecy of something impossible for anyone to know, or the bestowal of the gift of the Holy Spirit by the laying on of hands.

> According to Aquinas, the central function of miracles was to serve as a signum sensibile, a testimonium to guarantee the divine source and truth of Christian doctrines, particularly the deity of Christ. To explain the lack of visible miracles in his day, Aquinas asserted that Christ and his disciples had worked miracles sufficient to prove the faith once and for all; this having been done, no further miraculous proof of doctrines could be required.[46]

Interestingly, Aquinas, in contrast, allowed for the operation of miracles under certain circumstances:

> To confirm preaching and in the bringing of salvation to souls.[47]

Believers of great sanctity may operate in miraculous gifts of the Holy Spirit (which doctrine ironically "strengthened the veneration of shrines and canonization of saints via miracles...which essentially contradicted cessationism, [and] resulted in the excesses surrounding miracles which precipitated the Reformation.")[48]

In summary, we see developing significant Christian cessationist tenets during this period. As Ruthven points out, in the basics, they parallel those of the Jewish Rabbis:

> Spiritual power is normatively apportioned in descending tiers, at the idealized level of the biblical cannon versus the present time. The apostolic level of spiritual power could not, and likely should not, again be approached.[49]

> Only in a return to the (impossibly?) idealized righteousness of the New Testament could the church merit the charismata.[50]

> Miracles were once required as scaffolding for the church, which, once established (that is, in Scripture, tradition and institution), no longer required such support...Miracles and prophecy were replaced by piety and the study of Scripture.[51]

Cessationism and Calvinism

As we noted in the last section, the Roman Catholic Church had developed a heavily cessationist view in doctrine and practice, yet allowed that those of great sanctity could still operate in the miraculous, a view which, again, led to the veneration of shrines and the canonization of saints.

The Protestant reformers, in their quest to undermine the claims (based in the miraculous) of the Roman Catholic hierarchy, used that cessationist polemic against them. They also aimed it at "radical reformers" whose claims to the miraculous in establishing their own authority the Protestant reformers also sought to undermine.[52]

Chief among the reformers and significant to us is John Calvin. To better understand Calvin's effect on the development of Warfield's Polemic, we now want to focus on a brief summary of the key points of his cessationist doctrine in their historical context. Ruthven points out four significant aspects of the cessationist polemic of Calvinism which we quote and annotated with comments:[53]

> God's purpose for miracles was to accredit the word, that is, the Scripture, its doctrines and its first proclaimers. This proposition had the effect of restricting the power of accreditation by miracles to the major Protestant basis of religious authority: Scripture. This limitation to scripture and the original apostles of accrediting miracles was presented to undercut the religious authority of contemporary miracles thought to accredit the evolving doctrines and the contemporary leadership, derived from 'apostolic succession', of the Roman Church, as well as the 'Spirit-inspired' (and hence, religiously authoritative) teachings of the radical reformation.

Ruthven notes a quotation from Calvin which well illustrates the evidential argument of 'miracle' as authority on both sides:

> In demanding miracles of us they act dishonestly. For we are not forging some new gospel, but are retaining that very gospel whose truth all the miracles that Jesus Christ and his disciples ever run serve to confirm. But, compared with us, they have strange power: even to this day they can confirm their faith by continual miracles. Instead they allege miracles which can disturb a mind otherwise at rest—they are so foolish and ridiculous, so vain and false![54]

> Calvin uses the cessation evidential argument of 'miracle' to accredit his authority against the continuation evidential argument of 'miracle' by the Catholic leaders to accredit their authority.

> Counterfeit miracles are discerned by their association with false doctrines; hence, when miracles were claimed by the Catholics or the radical reformation as accrediting their unscriptural doctrines, such miracles were self-evidently false.

Comment: Observe the following portion from the previous quote which illustrates this point:

> '...they have strange power...they allege miracles which can disturb a mind otherwise at rest—they are so foolish and ridiculous, so vain and false!'[55]

> While 'visible', 'miraculous', 'extraordinary' or 'temporary' spiritual gifts ceased with the apostles, there is a possibility they may recur if conditions requiring their manifestation war-

> *rant. However, these types of spiritual gifts are more likely transmuted into the 'permanent' gifts and offices of contemporary Christian ministry or employed as metaphors for faith in the Gospel.*

Comment: Note that his cessationism is not as strict in this as other reformers. He essentially agrees with one of Aquinas' tenets for recurrence, to confirm preaching and in the bringing of salvation to souls.

> *What proof, other than his a priori association of miraculous charismata with accreditation of Scripture, does Calvin offer for their cessation? Surprisingly little: he appeals only superficially to Scripture and to the testimony of historical 'experience'. But in the main Calvin assumes the traditions enshrined in Aquinas, rather than attempt systematically to prove his contention.*

Comment: It is ironic that, according to Ruthven's study, Calvin (along with his "a priori association of miraculous charismata with the accreditation of Scripture") "appeals only superficially to Scripture and to the testimony of historical 'experience'" to prove his cessationist position. One of today's leading cessationist, Reformed voices, John F. MacArthur, in his book *Charismatic Chaos*, makes the following statement in reference to the "historical, objective" vs. "[charismatic] personal, subjective" "approach to biblical truth"[56]:

> *Objective, historic theology is Reformation theology. It is historical evangelicalism. It is historical orthodoxy. We begin with Scripture. Our thoughts, ideas, or experiences are validated or invalidated on the basis of how they compare with the Word.*[57]

His statements echo B. B. Warfield, who "defines Calvinism as the teachings of John Calvin, the Doctrinal System of the Reformed Churches"[58]:

> *There is no true religion in the world...which is not Calvinistic - Calvinistic in its essence, Calvinistic in its implication... in proportion as we are religious, in that proportion, then, are we Calvinistic; and when religion comes fully to its rights in our thinking, and feeling, and doing them shall we be truly Calvinistic...it is not merely the hope of true religion in the world: it is true religion in the world—as far as true religion is in the world at all.*[59]

Is it possible that Warfield's (and his echoes') Calvinistic, Reformed cessationist foundation of "true religion" does not all "begin with Scripture," that the "thoughts, ideas, or experiences" behind the cessationist position that are supposedly "validated or invalidated on the basis of how they compare with the Word" are not actually so validated?

For more teaching/understanding on the refutation of such thinking, listen or watch Dr. Clark's series, "Biblical and Historical Answers to Cessationism."

Endnotes

> [1]Jon Ruthven, On the Cessation of the Charismata: The Protestant Polemic on Postbiblical Miracles Journal of Pentecostal Theology Supplement Series 3 (Sheffield, England: Sheffield Academic Press Ltd, 1993, 1997) p. 14

²Vinson Synan, *In the Latter Days* (Fairfax, VA: Xulon Press, 2001) pp. 134-135

³*Ibid.* p. 82

⁴Jon Ruthven, *On the Cessation of the Charismata: The Protestant Polemic on Postbiblical Miracles Journal of Pentecostal Theology Supplement Series 3* (Sheffield, England: Sheffield Academic Press Ltd, 1993, 1997) p. 14

⁵*Ibid.* p. 15

⁶*Ibid.* pp. 15-16, footnote 3

⁷John F. MacArthur, Jr., *Charismatic Chaos* (Grand Rapids, MI: Zondervan, 1992) p. 18

⁸*Ibid.* p. 19

⁹Jon Ruthven, *On the Cessation of the Charismata: The Protestant Polemic on Postbiblical Miracles Journal of Pentecostal Theology Supplement Series 3* (Sheffield, England: Sheffield Academic Press Ltd, 1993, 1997) pp. 18-20

¹⁰*Ibid.* p. 20

¹¹*Ibid.* pp. 21-20

¹²Jon Ruthven, *On the Cessation of the Charismata: The Protestant Polemic on Postbiblical Miracles Journal of Pentecostal Theology Supplement Series 3* (Sheffield, England: Sheffield Academic Press Ltd, 1993, 1997) pp 22-23, footnote 1

¹³plural of cha•ris•ma [Greek charisma favor, gift, from charizesthai to favor, from charis grace, an extraordinary power (as of healing) given a Christian by the Holy Spirit for the good of the church, from *Merriam-Webster's Collegiate Dictionary*, 10th edition (Springfield, MA: MerriamWebster, 1996)

¹⁴Jon Ruthven, *On the Cessation of the Charismata: The Protestant Polemic on Postbiblical Miracles Journal of Pentecostal Theology Supplement Series 3* (Sheffield, England: Sheffield Academic Press Ltd, 1993, 1997) p.16, the continuation of footnote 3, p. 15

¹⁵*Ibid.* pp. 23, 189

¹⁶*Ibid.* p. 23

¹⁷*Ibid.* p. 23

¹⁸*Ibid.* p. 24

¹⁹*Ibid.* pp. 24-25

²⁰*Ibid.*

²¹*Ibid.* p. 25, footnote 1

²²*Ibid.* p. 25

²³*Ibid.*

²⁴*Ibid.* p. 26

[25] Ibid. p. 31

[26] Ibid. p. 27, the continuation of footnote 4, p. 26

[27] Ibid.

[28] Theological dictionary of the New Testament. 1964-c1976. Vols. 5-9 edited by Gerhard Friedrich. Vol. 10 compiled by Ronald Pitkin. (G. Kittel, G. W. Bromiley & G. Friedrich, Ed.) (electronic ed.) (Vol. 6, Page 383). Grand Rapids, MI: Eerdmans.7276 Str.-B., II, 130. 8277 Tanch. 231a; Nu. r., 20, 1 on 22:2 (Str.-B., II, 130). Acc. to other sayings it took place when Israel had received the Torah, Seder Olam Rabba, 21 (Str.-B., II, 130) or after the completion of the tabernacle, Cant. r., 2:3 R. Jishaq.

[29] Jon Ruthven, On the Cessation of the Charismata: The Protestant Polemic on Postbiblical Miracles Journal of Pentecostal Theology Supplement Series 3 (Sheffield, England: Sheffield Academic Press Ltd, 1993, 1997) p. 27, the continuation of footnote 4, p. 26

[30] Ibid. p. 27

[31] Gordon D. Fee, The First Epistle to the Corinthians, NICNT (Grand Rapids, MI: Eerdmans, 1987), p. 645, footnote 23, (2)

[32] Arndt, W., Danker, F. W., & Bauer, W. (2000). A Greek-English lexicon of the New Testament and other early Christian literature. "Based on Walter Bauer's Griechisch-deutsches Writerbuch zu den Schriften des Neuen Testaments und der frhüchristlichen [sic] Literatur, sixth edition, ed. Kurt Aland and Barbara Aland, with Viktor Reichmann and on previous English editions by W.F. Arndt, F.W. Gingrich, and F.W. Danker." (3rd ed.) (Page 974). Chicago: University of Chicago Press.

[33] Jon Ruthven, On the Cessation of the Charismata: The Protestant Polemic on Postbiblical Miracles Journal of Pentecostal Theology Supplement Series 3 (Sheffield, England: Sheffield Academic Press Ltd, 1993, 1997) p. 28

[34] Ibid. p. 28, footnote 1

[35] Ibid. p. 29

[36] Ibid.

[37] Ibid.

[38] Ibid.

[39] Ibid. pp. 29-30.

[40] Ibid. p 30

[41] Ibid. p. 31

[42] Ibid. p. 31, footnote 1

⁴³*Ibid. p. 31*

⁴⁴*Ibid.*

⁴⁵*Ibid.*

⁴⁶*Ibid. pp. 32-33*

⁴⁷*Ibid. p. 33*

⁴⁸*Ibid. p. 33*

⁴⁹*Ibid. p. 30*

⁵⁰*Ibid. pp. 30-31*

⁵¹*Ibid. p. 31*

⁵²*Ibid. p. 33*

⁵³*Ibid. pp. 34-35*

⁵⁴*Ibid. p 35, footnote 1, cited from Institutes, Prefatory Address. 3 (16)*

⁵⁵*Ibid.*

⁵⁶*John F. MacArthur, Jr., Charismatic Chaos (Grand Rapids, MI: Zondervan, 1992) p. 36*

⁵⁷*Ibid.*

⁵⁸*Jon Ruthven, On the Cessation of the Charismata: The Protestant Polemic on Postbiblical Miracles Journal of Pentecostal Theology Supplement Series 3 (Sheffield, England: Sheffield Academic Press Ltd, 1993, 1997) pp. 39-40, footnote 2*

In this next section we will review Biblical doctrines contrary to the doctrine of Cessationism based on Ruthven's Polemic on the subject and his review of Warfield's "Counterfeit Miracles":

Ruthven identifies two biblical doctrines which are contradictory to Warfield's cessation position, the doctrine of the Holy Spirit and the doctrine of the Kingdom of God.

The Doctrine of the Holy Spirit

Warfield's cessationist view of the post-canonical activity of the Holy Spirit being limited to the "Calvinistic concepts of regeneration and sanctification" is in keeping with Calvinistic view of the exalted Christ:

When the revelation of God in Christ had taken place, and had become in Scripture and church a constituent part of the cosmos, then another era began...Christ has come, His work has been done, and His word is complete.

God the Holy Spirit has made it his subsequent work, not to introduce new and unneeded revelations into the world, but to defuse this one complete revelation to the world and to bring mankind into saving knowledge of it.[1]

As Ruthven observes:

The exalted Christ seems presently inactive, waiting, it appears, for the preaching of Calvinistic soteriology to accomplish its task in the world...These representative statements of theological doctrine seen to reflect more of an urgency to protect the authority of Scripture than to describe carefully its teaching.[2] Warfield failed "to grasp the characteristic biblical activity of the Spirit that is so inimical [contrary] to cessationism" and "the fact that Scripture repeatedly emphasizes the promise of the universal outpouring of this Spirit of prophecy and miracle on 'all people'...not simply to accredit apostles and those 'upon whom apostolic hands were laid', but to all future generations, conditional only upon repentance and faith. The Bible sees the outpouring of the Spirit and his gifts upon the church as characteristic of the age of the messiah and his reign in the kingdom of God."[3]

Ruthven reports how he followed the steps of Warfield's principles of interpretation, classifying every biblical reference to the Holy Spirit according to "any contextual description". In the Old Testament, "of the 128 appearances, 76 primarily described prophetic or revelatory activities of the Spirit; 18 were charismatic leadership; 14 were divine (miraculous) power; and 18 were the sustenance of life;" He reports finding similar proportions in the more numerous references to the Spirit in the New Testament.[4]

The Doctrine of the Kingdom of God

In his research, Ruthven identified "several key theological aspects of the kingdom of God" for which Warfield failed "to grasp the charismatic significance"[5]:

- His "picture of Jesus' earthly and exalted mission...fails to show Christ as the continuing source of the charismata among those who would receive them."[6]

- His Calvinistic soteriology "is limited to the problem of sin" and "fails to grasp the holistic nature of salvation, including healing, revelation and deliverance from demonic power."[7]

- His eschatology "is flawed" because Warfield "fails to see the work of the kingdom of God (alternatively, the Spirit of God) as biblically described, that is, that the exalted Christ be stows charismata provisionally in this age as a 'down payment', the 'first fruits', or a 'taste of the powers of the age to come'.[8]

Ruthven contrasts, the former "two-part schema shared by the Old Testament and the rabbis, which divided history into...this present age (from creation to the coming of the messiah), and the age to come (the coming of the messiah onward)"⁹ with the Church age:

> *The New Testament saw the two ages as overlapping: the coming of the messiah, Jesus inaugurated the time of the kingdom and Spirit in the opening victories over the kingdom of Satan…. [Christ's exaltation and the outpouring of the Spirit] expanded this conflict, through the ministry of the church, a conflict characterized by the restoration of hearts, souls and bodies from the control of the kingdom of darkness-, via the preaching of the word and through healings and miracles."*[10]

He adds further:

> *The New Testament expressly ties the presence of the charismata to the exalted Lordship of Jesus…God, through his exalted Christ in his church, continues his earthly ministry of deliverance through the church (John 7.39; 16.7, 17). The 'greater works' of those who believe in him can be performed only because Jesus goes to his Father (Jn 14.12, cf. Acts 2.33, 36b, 38-39)."*[11]

Finally, Ruthven says of Raymond Brown:

> *[He] represents the consensus of modern biblical scholarship when he writes: 'Jesus' miracles were not only primarily external confirmation of his message; rather than miracle was the vehicle of the message. Side by side, word and miraculous deed gave expression to the entrance of God's kingly power into time.*[12]

Biblical Passages Demonstrating the Continuation of the Charismata

In his analyses of these passages, Ruthven step-by-step applies Warfield's principles of interpretation to exegete them, provides in his summary paraphrases based on his exegesis. While an in-depth study is beyond our means in this course, we will highlight common themes and encourage you to investigate it further on your own.

Common Themes

- The Charismata are Christ "centric."

They are given by God through the exalted Christ Jesus, continuously to confirm the 'testimony of Christ', until the Lord Jesus Christ is revealed, in the 'day of the Lord Jesus Christ'.[13]

- The Charismata are "not granted to exalt the self-centered."

"The abundance of charismata serve usefully to promote maturity in believers throughout the present age, but these gifts will be overwhelmed and replaced by the consummation of the age, the 'and', the kingdom in its fullness, that is, the revelation of our Lord Jesus Christ in the 'day' of his glory."

- The Charismata are eschatological.

"Spiritual gifts express the contemporary presence of the future kingdom of God."

- They are not earned, but are God's "grace" and "graces."
- They are for the purpose of confirming/strengthening believers.[14]

Key Passages

> **1 Corinthians 13:8-12**
>
> Love never fails; but if there are gifts of prophecy, they will be done away; if there are tongues, they will cease; if there is knowledge, it will be done away. For we know in part and we prophesy in part; but when the perfect comes, the partial will be done away. When I was a child, I used to speak like a child, think like a child, reason like a child; when I became a man, I did away with childish things. For now we see in a mirror dimly, but then face to face; now I know in part, but then I will know fully just as I also have been fully known. (NASB95)

Chart from of Ruthven's analysis of this passage showing the contrasting aspects of the present and future age[15]

Verses 9-10	Verse 11	Verse 12	Verse 12
(Now our) Knowledge is imperfect prophecy is imperfect	I used to speak as a child, think as a child, reason as a child	Now I see dimly, indirectly	Now I know in part
when the perfect comes the imperfect will be ended	when I became a man I gave up infantile things	then I shall know, see face to face	then I shall know as fully as I am known

> **1 Corinthians 1:4-8**
>
> I thank my God always concerning you for the grace of God which was given you in Christ Jesus, that in everything you were [past] enriched in Him, in all speech [verbal charismata] and all knowledge [revelatory charismata], even as the testimony concerning Christ was confirmed in you, so that you are [present] not lacking in any gift [charisma], awaiting eagerly the revelation of our Lord Jesus Christ, who will [future] also confirm you to the end [completion of the age], blameless in the day of our Lord Jesus Christ. (NASB95)

> **Ephesians 4:7-13**
>
> But to each one of us grace was given according to the measure of Christ's gift. Therefore it says, "When He ascended on high, He led captive a host of captives, And He gave gifts to men." (Now this expression, "He ascended," what does it mean except that He also had descended into the lower parts of the earth? He who descended is Himself also He who ascended far above all the heavens, so that He might fill all things.) And He gave some as apostles, and some as prophets, and some as evangelists, and some as pastors and teachers, for the equipping of the saints for the work of service, to the building up of the body of Christ; until we all attain to the unity of the faith, and of the knowledge of the Son of God, to a mature man, to the measure of the stature which belongs to the fullness of Christ. (NASB95)

Auxiliary Passages which reiterate the key passage

Even a basic perusal of the following passages reveals exhortation and expectation to seek for, pray for, live in, and operate in kingdom power dynamics until Christ's return. These verses are filled with themes such as:

> *Receiving his grace and power and glory, being filled up to all the fullness of God, being clothed with power, having power together with all the saints, praying for all wisdom and spiritual understanding, being empowered, the gifts (charismata) and calling of God are irrevocable, the proclamation of the Gospel in word and deed, don't quench the Spirit, do works of faith in power, preserved by the power of God, Be prepared for Christ's return in power and glory.*

> **Romans 11:29**
>
> For God's gifts [charismata] and his call are irrevocable.

> **Ephesians 1: 13-14, 17-21**
>
> And you also were included in Christ when you heard the word of truth, the gospel of your salvation. Having believed, you were marked in him with a seal, the promised Holy Spirit, who is a deposit guaranteeing our inheritance until the redemption of those who are God's possession - to the praise of his glory.

Ephesians 1:17-21

I keep asking that the God of our Lord Jesus Christ, the glorious Father, may give you the Spirit of wisdom and revelation, so that you may know him better. I pray also that the eyes of your heart may be enlightened in order that you may know the hope to which he has called you, the riches of his glorious inheritance in the saints, and his incomparably great power for us who believe. That power is like the working of his mighty strength, which he exerted in Christ when he raised him from the dead and seated him at his right hand in the heavenly realms, far above all rule and authority, power and dominion, and every title that can be given, not only in the present age but also in the one to come.

Ephesians 3:14-21

For this reason I kneel before the Father, from whom his whole family in heaven and on earth derives its name. I pray that out of his glorious riches he may strengthen you with power through his Spirit in your inner being, so that Christ may dwell in your hearts through faith. And I pray that you, being rooted and established in love, may have power, together with all the saints, to grasp how wide and long and high and deep is the love of Christ, and to know this love that surpasses knowledge—that you may be filled to the measure of all the fullness of God. Now to him who is able to do immeasurably more than all we ask or imagine, according to his power that is at work within us, to him be glory in the church and in Christ Jesus throughout all generations, for ever and ever! Amen.

Ephesians 4:30

And do not grieve the Holy Spirit of God, with whom you were sealed for the day of redemption. (NIV)

Ephesians 5:15-19

Be very careful, then, how you live—not as unwise but as wise, making the most of every opportunity, because the days are evil. Therefore do not be foolish, but understand what the Lord's will is. Do not get drunk on wine, which leads to debauchery. Instead, be filled with the Spirit. Speak to one another with psalms, hymns and spiritual songs. Sing and make music in your heart to the Lord.

Ephesians 6:10-20

Finally, be strong in the Lord and in his mighty power. Put on the full armor of God so that you can take your stand against the devil's schemes. For our struggle is not against flesh and blood, but against the rulers, against the authorities, against the powers of this dark world and against the spiritual forces of evil in the heavenly realms. Therefore put on the full armor of God, so that when the day of evil comes, you may be able to stand your ground, and after you have done everything, to stand. Stand firm then, with the belt of truth buckled around your waist, with the breastplate of righteousness in place, and with your feet fitted with the readiness that comes from the gospel of peace. In addition to all this, take up the shield of faith, with which you can extinguish all the flaming arrows of the evil one. Take the helmet of salvation and the sword of the Spirit, which is the word of God. And pray in the Spirit on all occasions with all kinds of prayers and requests. With this in mind, be alert and always keep on praying for all the saints. Pray also for me, that whenever I open my mouth, words may be given me so that I will fearlessly make known the mystery of the gospel, for which I am an ambassador in chains. Pray that I may declare it fearlessly, as I should.

Philippians 1:9-10

And this is my prayer: that your love may abound more and more in knowledge and depth of insight, so that you may be able to discern what is best and may be pure and blameless until the day of Christ.

Colossians 1:9-12

For this reason, since the day we heard about you, we have not stopped praying for you and asking God to fill you with the knowledge of his will through all spiritual wisdom and understanding. And we pray this in order that you may live a life worthy of the Lord and may please him in every way: bearing fruit in every good work, growing in the knowledge of God, being strengthened with all power according to his glorious might so that you may have great endurance and patience, and joyfully giving thanks to the Father, who has qualified you to share in the inheritance of the saints in the kingdom of light.

1 Thessalonians 1:5-8

Because our gospel came to you not simply with words, but also with power, with the Holy Spirit and with deep conviction. You know how we lived among you for your sake. You became imitators of us and of the Lord; in spite of severe suffering, you welcomed the message with the joy given by the Holy Spirit. And so you became a model to all the believers in Macedonia and Achaia. The Lord's message rang out from you not only in Macedonia and Achaia— your faith in God has become known everywhere. Therefore we do not need to say anything about it.

1 Thessalonians 5:11-23

Therefore encourage one another and build each other up, just as in fact you are doing. Now we ask you, brothers, to respect those who work hard among you, who are over you in the Lord and who admonish you. Hold them in the highest regard in love because of their work. Live in peace with each other. And we urge you, brothers, warn those who are idle, encourage the timid, help the weak, be patient with everyone. Make sure that nobody pays back wrong for wrong, but always try to be kind to each other and to everyone else. Be joyful always; pray continually; give thanks in all circumstances, for this is God's will for you in Christ Jesus. Do not put out the Spirit's fire; do not treat prophecies with contempt. Test everything. Hold on to the good. Avoid every kind of evil. May God himself, the God of peace, sanctify you through and through. May your whole spirit, soul and body be kept blameless at the coming of our Lord Jesus Christ.

2 Thessalonians 1:11-12

With this in mind, we constantly pray for you, that our God may count you worthy of his calling, and that by his power he may fulfill every good purpose of yours and every act prompted by your faith. We pray this so that the name of our Lord Jesus may be glorified in you, and you in him, according to the grace of our God and the Lord Jesus Christ.

1 Peter 1:5

Who through faith are shielded by God's power until the coming of the salvation that is ready to be revealed in the last time.

1 Peter 4:7-12

The end of all things is near. Therefore be clear minded and self-controlled so that you can pray. Above all, love each other deeply, because love covers over a multitude of sins. Offer hospitality to one another without grumbling. Each one should use whatever gift he has received to serve others, faithfully administering God's grace in its various forms. If anyone speaks, he should do it as one speaking the very words of God. If anyone serves, he should do it with the strength God provides, so that in all things God may be praised through Jesus Christ. To him be the glory and the power for ever and ever. Amen. Dear friends, do not be surprised at the painful trial you are suffering, as though something strange were happening to you.

> **1 John 2:26-28**
>
> I am writing these things to you about those who are trying to lead you astray. As for you, the anointing you received from him remains in you, and you do not need anyone to teach you. But as his anointing teaches you about all things and as that anointing is real, not counterfeit— just as it has taught you, remain in him. And now, dear children, continue in him, so that when he appears we may be confident and unashamed before him at his coming.
>
> **Jude 18-21**
>
> They said to you, "In the last times there will be scoffers who will follow their own ungodly desires." These are the men who divide you, who follow mere natural instincts and do not have the Spirit. But you, dear friends, build yourselves up in your most holy faith and pray in the Holy Spirit. Keep yourselves in God's love as you wait for the mercy of our Lord Jesus Christ to bring you to eternal life.

Final Remarks

An excellent closing summary to this portion of our study is an astute, articulate analysis by Southern Baptist scholar Dr. Robert H. Culpepper from his work *Evaluating the Charismatic Movement: A Theological and Biblical Appraisal*:

> *The first task is that of seeking to discover if there is any sound basis for distinguishing some gifts as temporary and others as permanent. We should note that this type of thinking has never been a part of Catholic thought. Indeed, one of the prerequisites for the canonization of a saint in Catholic life is that there must be strong attestation that the person so canonized has worked miracles. Catholics, they, have not ordinarily rejected offhand the possibility of contemporary miracles. Rather, they have tended to think of the medium through which they operate as being not ordinary Christians, but "saints" in their special understanding of the word.*
>
> *When we come to Protestantism, however, we find a different picture. There is a tendency to stress the temporary character of some of the gifts. One view is that the purpose of the miracle or sign gifts was to authenticate the Christian message in the days before the completion of Scripture. Now that the canon of Scripture has been completed, there is no longer a need for further display of the miraculous gifts. In the Pauline sense, they say, we no longer have apostles and prophets in our day. Neither are the gifts of miracles, healing, tongues, interpretation of tongues, and discerning of spirits in evidence. All these were temporary gifts never intended for the permanent life of the church. Those who take this view usually cite 1 Corinthians 13:8-9 in its support. Here it is said that Paul maintains that tongues and prophecy will pass away when the perfect is come. They usually interpret "that which is perfect" as referring to the Bible.*

Another view is that the purpose of the special supernatural gifts was the authentication of the apostles. Thus, we are told, some of those upon whom the apostles laid their hands received miracle-working power, but they were not able to pass this along to others. Miracles then inevitably passed from the scene with the death of the apostles and their disciples. In support of this view passages that emphasize miracles as authenticating the apostles are cited (Acts 14:3; Romans 15:18-19; 2 Corinthians 12:12; Hebrews 2:3-4). Those who take this view sometimes assert that nowhere does the New Testament tell us that we are to continue to manifest the miraculous gifts. Sometimes the proponents of this theory fuse it with the first view in saying that the disappearance of the miraculous gifts is not great loss to the church, because we now have the complete Bible. To insist that the church still needs miraculous signs today, they say, is to overlook the finality of the Scriptures.

In at least one of these gifts the distinction between the temporary and the permanent is valid. We no longer have apostles today in the sense of those who as witnesses to the resurrection and the recipients of God's primal revelation laid the foundation for the Christian church for all ages (Acts 1:22; Ephesians 2:20). The recognition of this fact, however, does not provide a solid basis for making the type of broad distinction between the so-called miraculous and nonmiraculous gifts that is outlined in the theories described above. [Author's note: I agree there are not to be Apostles who have the authority to write new Scripture or who are on a standing with the 12, but there is another class, order, type of apostle in the Bible that seems to be similar to a church planting missionary who moves in powerful gifts of the Holy Spirit. This type of apostle still exists today in the church and has never dropped out of the existence of the Church.

It seems to me that these theories will not stand for two reasons. First, they are not well grounded biblically. It is poor exegesis to appeal to 1 Corinthians 13:8-9 in support of the idea that tongues and prophecy are temporary, for in the context of that passage "that which is perfect" refers not to the completed Scriptures, but to the complete revelation of Christ which will come when we see him "face to face." [Author's note: F.F. Bruce, a famous Evangelical scholar makes the exact point in his commentary on 1 Corinthians.] A misunderstanding is manifest also in the interpretation of the purpose of miracles and spiritual gifts that is expressed. Not only did the miracles of Jesus bear witness to the fact that he was the Christ, the bearer of the kingdom, but also they gave expression to the compassion of Jesus. Such compassion was manifest also in most of the miracles performed by the apostles through the Spirit. [Emphasis added] The New Testament affirms that the new age has dawned, that the kingdom is a present reality. If that is true today, we have no basis for dismissing miracles out of court. Paul speaks of the spiritual gifts that are in dispute as having been given by the Spirit for edification of the body of Christ. If those gifts served to edify the body then, what basis do we have for thinking they could not bring edification in our day? Some interpreters who insist on the temporary character of the miraculous gifts say that the New Testament nowhere promises that these gifts will continue. This argument can be turned around. Nowhere does it say that they will not continue. Rather, the implication is that they will, for, according to John 14:12, Jesus promised that his disciples would continue his works and do even greater ones, and Hebrews 13:8 says that "Jesus Christ is the same yesterday and today and forever."

A second reason for rejecting the theory of the temporary nature of the gifts is that there is good evidence for believing that the Holy Spirit still bestows his gifts upon his people when there is an attitude of openness and expectancy. I once viewed the miraculous manifestations of the Spirit as temporary in design and expressed this view in an article on "The Problem of Miracles" in the April 1956, issue of the Review and Expositor. [Author's note: This is the scholarly publication of Southern Baptist Theological Seminary, Louisville, Ky.] However, what I have seen, heard, read, thought, felt and experienced since then has convinced me that I was wrong. When fact and theory collide, the better part of wisdom is to revise or discard the theory in the light of the facts rather than stubbornly to hold to the theory in defiance of the facts. In my judgment, views of the temporary nature of the gifts should be buried.[16]

Summary

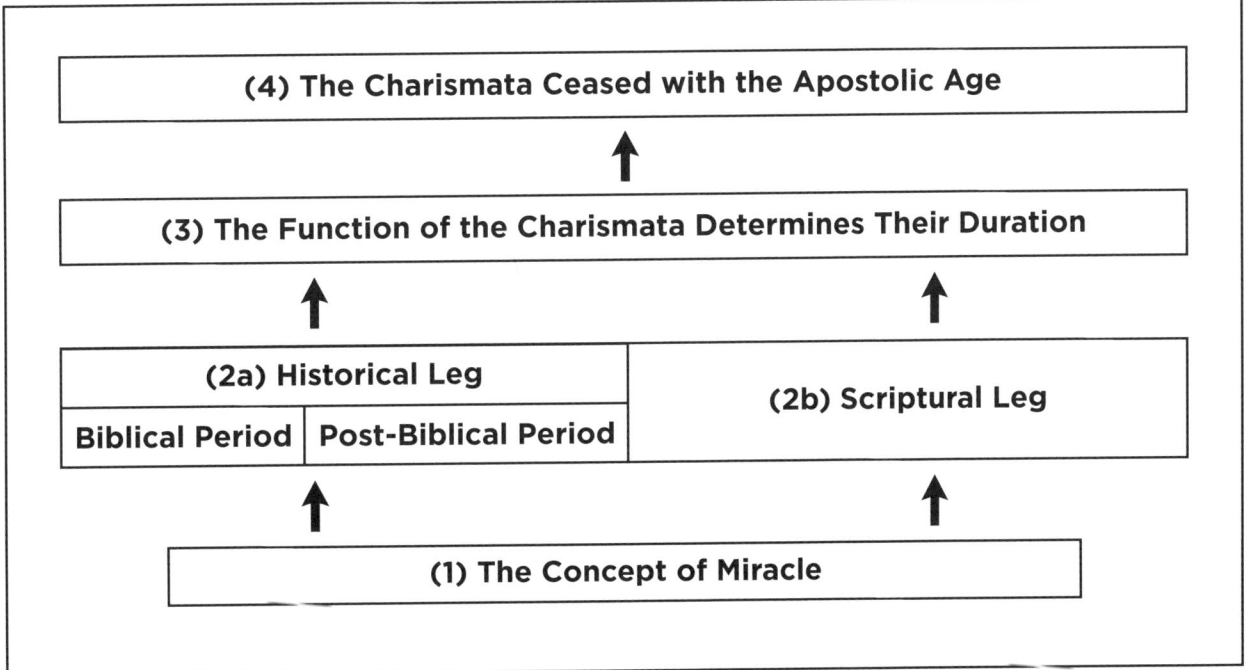

In this section we have examined the (2b) Scriptural "leg" of Warfield's cessationist polemic by analyzing the nature and application of his methodology of biblical interpretation. It joins his concept of miracle (1) and historical methodology (2a) in being flawed.

We conclude that the evidence is clear that B.B. Warfield's cessationist, evidential view of the Charismata is fatally flawed, and that the Charismata did not cease with the Apostolic age.

In addition, we have shown strong evidence that Warfield's own principles of interpretation - minus his cessationist presuppositions - when honestly and consistently applied to Scripture lead to this conclusion - that the function of the charismata is to express the Gospel of the Kingdom and that their continued operation is intrinsic to its full and complete proclamation until Christ returns.

In the remaining lessons of this series, we will survey a history of the operation of the charismata throughout Church history which bear testimony to the conclusion that the gifts have not ceased, but continue as an expression of the Kingdom of God on earth.

Endnotes

[1] *Jon Ruthven, On the Cessation of the Charismata: The Protestant Polemic on Postbiblical Miracles Journal of Pentecostal Theology Supplement Series 3 (Sheffield, England: Sheffield Academic Press Ltd, 1993, 1997) Ibid. p. 112-188*

[2] *Ibid. p. 114*

[3] *Ibid. p. 113, footnote 1 citation: Warfield, Counterfeit Miracles, p. 28*

[4] *Ibid. pp. 112-113, footnote 1 citation: Warfield, Counterfeit Miracles, p. 26*

[5] *Ibid. p. 113*

[6] *Ibid. p. 115*

[7] *Ibid. pp. 114-115, footnote 2*

[8] *Ibid. p. 119*

[9] *Ibid.*

[10] *Ibid.*

[11] *Ibid.*

[12] *Ibid.*

[13] *Ibid. p 121*

[14] *Ibid.*

[15] *Ibid p. 116, footnote 2.*

[16] *Ibid. p. 125*

NOTES

NOTES

CHAPTER 16

HEALING AND THE GLORY OF GOD

LESSON GOALS

1. To gain a Biblical understanding of the Glory of God.
2. To examine the Glory of God as it relates to signs and wonders, miracles and healing.
3. To look at how Jesus Glorified the Father, and manifested the Father's Glory.
4. To consider the place of the Glory of God for today as it relates to our own walks.

INTRODUCTION

In this lesson we will be discussing the Glory of God as it relates to moving in signs, wonders, the miraculous, and healing. To emphasize the reality and significance of what we are going to discuss, I would like to share some current testimonies from ministries experiencing the Glory of God and the miraculous.

Illustrations:

- Heidi and Mark in Mozambique: the Shamans and the Muslim cleric's conversion
- Doug Oss in Utah: the instantaneous healings
- Raleigh, North Carolina: The Glory Cloud

KEY INSIGHTS

The Glory: Gaining a Biblical Understanding

O. T. Word Study of the Hebrew Word for Glory

This word study is condensed from Brown-Driver-Briggs Hebrew and English Lexicon, Hendrickson Publishing, 1996.

- כבוֹד (kabōd): adjective, glorious, noun, abundance, honor, glory

- abundance, riches Gen. 31:1, Is. 10:3; 61:6; 66:11, 12 Na. 2:10 Psalm 49:17, 18.

- honour, splendour, glory of God, glory, in historic theophanies: to Moses Ex. 33:18, 22;

- for theophanies of the Exodus 16:7, 10; 24:16, 17; 40:34, 35 Lv. 9:6, 23 Nu. 14:10; 16:19; 17:7; 2:6, cf. 2 Ch. 5:14 = 1 K. 8:11, 2 Ch 7:1, 2, 3; so Ezek., Ez. 1:28; 3:12, 23

- Ezekiel 3:23
- Exodus 29:43
- Psalm 26:8
- Isaiah 4:5
- Isaiah 6:3
- Psalm 19
- Psalm 24:7, 8, 9, 10
- Psalm 102:16
- Isaiah 40:5
- Isaiah 35:2
- Ezekiel 43:2
- Isaiah 58:8
- Isaiah 60:1, 2
- Haggai 2:7
- Habakkuk 2:14
- Psalm 72:19
- Isaiah 66:18, 19
- Psalm 97:6
- Psalm 102:16
- Isaiah 59:19

N. T. Word Study of the Greek Word for Glory

Note: this word study was condensed from a *Greek-English Lexicon of the New Testament and other Early Christian Literature* by Bauer, Arndt and Gingrich, Edited by Danker, University of Chicago Press, 2001.

Noun: δοξα, ης, (doxa):

- The condition of being bright or shining, brightness, splendor, radiance (a distinctive aspect of Hebrew Kabod (כבוד): I could not see because of the brightness of the light

- Acts 22:11; see the radiance Lk. 9:32

- Everything in heaven has this radiance: the radiant bodies in the sky 1 Cor 15:40f
- Of humans involved in transcendent circumstances, and also transcendent beings
- Cherubim Heb. 9:5
- Angels Lk. 2:9; Rev. 18:1
- Especially of God's self (Ex. 24:17; 40:34; Num. 14:10 Acts 7:2 (Ps 28:3); cp. Jn. 12:41 (Is. 6:1); Ac 7:55; 2 Th. 1:9; 2 Pt. 1:17b; Rev. 15:8; 19:1; 21:11, 23, (the Father of Glory) Eph. 1:17
- The state of being in the next life is described as participation in the radiance or glory
- A state of being magnificent, greatness, splendor
- A transcendent being deserving of honor, majestic being
- δοξαζω (doxazo): verb, to cause to have splendid greatness, clothe in splendor, glorify
- It is a favorite term in John in which the whole life of Jesus is depicted as a glorifying of the Son by the Father: Jn. 8:54; 12:28; 13:31; 17:1, 4 and, at the same time, of the Father by the Son: Jn. 13:31f; 14:13; 17:1. The glorifying of the Son is brought about by the miracles which the Father has him perform.

Eighteen Associations with Glory in the Bible (Not exhaustive study, but selective)

- Glory associated with a cloud – Reference(s): 23
- Glory associated with fire – Reference(s): 11
- Glory connected to healings – Reference(s): 16 (including implications)
- Glory connected with miracles – Reference(s): 14 (including implications)
- Glory used as a synonym for power – Reference(s): 9
- Glory associated with future state of existence in presence of God – Reference(s): 12
- Glory connected to Judgment – Reference(s): 5
- Glory associated with ministry to the poor – Reference(s): 1
- Glory associated with revelation of God's name – Reference(s): 1
- Glory caused things to be consecrated – Reference(s): 1
- Glory connected to God's house – Reference(s): 3
- God receives Glory through the worship of all nations or all nations shall see his glory – Reference(s): 8

- God's glory associated with Angels – Reference(s): 7 (N.T. only)

- What God told Moses to do in order to see His glory. – Reference(s): 1 (Lev. 9:6-7)

- God gained glory for himself by extending the borders of Israel. – Reference(s): 1

- Glory appeared like illuminated rainbow – Reference(s): 1

- Glory appeared as light, radiance – Reference(s): 8

- Glory associated with suffering – Reference(s): 8

- Glory to deep to comprehend – Reference(s): 1

Focusing on the Relationship of Glory to Healing and Miracles

We want to take a brief survey in Scripture on the relationship of glory to healing and miracles through the writings of Moses, the prophet Isaiah, and the apostles John, Paul and Peter. It is "Christ in you, the hope of glory" which empowers for healing and miracles.

The Prophet and Lawgiver Moses

1. Miraculous provision of quail.

> **Exodus 16:4-14**
>
> Then the Lord said to Moses, "I will rain down bread from heaven for you. The people are to go out each day and gather enough for that day. In this way I will test them and see whether they will follow my instructions. On the sixth day they are to prepare what they bring in, and that is to be twice as much as they gather on the other days." So Moses and Aaron said to all the Israelites, "In the evening you will know that it was the Lord who brought you out of Egypt, and in the morning you will see the glory of the Lord, because he has heard your grumbling against him. Who are we, that you should grumble against us?" Moses also said, "You will know that it was the Lord when he gives you meat to eat in the evening and all the bread you want in the morning, because he has heard your grumbling against him. Who are we? You are not grumbling against us, but against the Lord." Then Moses told Aaron, "Say to the entire Israelite community, 'Come before the Lord, for he has heard your grumbling.'" While Aaron was speaking to the whole Israelite community, they looked toward the desert, and there was the glory of the Lord appearing in the cloud. The Lord said to Moses, "I have heard the grumbling of the Israelites. Tell them, 'At twilight you will eat meat, and in the morning you will be filled with bread. Then you will know that I am the Lord your God.'" That evening quail came and covered the camp, and in the morning there was a layer of dew around the camp. When the dew was gone, thin flakes like frost on the ground appeared on the desert floor.

> **Numbers 20:6-12**
>
> Moses and Aaron went from the assembly to the entrance to the Tent of Meeting and fell facedown, and the glory of the Lord appeared to them. The Lord said to Moses, "Take the staff, and you and your brother Aaron gather the assembly together. Speak to that rock before their eyes and it will pour out its water. You will bring water out of the rock for the community so they and their livestock can drink." So Moses took the staff from the Lord's presence, just as he commanded him. He and Aaron gathered the assembly together in front of the rock and Moses said to them, "Listen, you rebels, must we bring you water out of this rock?" Then Moses raised his arm and struck the rock twice with his staff. Water gushed out, and the community and their livestock drank. But the Lord said to Moses and Aaron, "Because you did not trust in me enough to honor me as holy in the sight of the Israelites, you will not bring this community into the land I give them."

2. Miraculous supply of water from a rock.

Illustrations:

- Heidi and Rolland Baker and the multiplication of bread for refugees.
- William Branham who had to obey what he saw in the vision exactly as seen for Betty Daugherty's healing to occur.

The Prophet Isaiah – Ministry to the Poor, Glory and Healing

> **Isaiah 58:6-12**
>
> Is not this the kind of fasting I have chosen: to loose the chains of injustice and untie the cords of the yoke, to set the oppressed free and break every yoke? Is it not to share your food with the hungry and to provide the poor wanderer with shelter— when you see the naked, to clothe him, and not to turn away from your own flesh and blood? Then your light will break forth like the dawn, and your healing will quickly appear; then your righteousness will go before you, and the glory of the Lord will be your rear guard. Then you will call, and the Lord will answer; you will cry for help, and he will say: Here am I. If you do away with the yoke of oppression, with the pointing finger and malicious talk, and if you spend yourselves in behalf of the hungry and satisfy the needs of the oppressed, then your light will rise in the darkness, and your night will become like the noonday. The Lord will guide you always; he will satisfy your needs in a sun-scorched land and will strengthen your frame. You will be like a well-watered garden, like a spring whose waters never fail. Your people will rebuild the ancient ruins and will raise up the age-old foundations; you will be called Repairer of Broken Walls, Restorer of Streets with Dwellings.

There is a connection between ministering to the poor and glory and healing:

Illustration:

The greatest miracle stories occur while working among the poor. As an example, Heidi and Rolland Baker working among the poor in Mozambique, Africa have seen the blind see, the deaf hear, the lame walk, the dead raised, a plague of cholera stopped, food multiplied and other supernatural provision.

The Father and the Son are Glorified Through Miracles and Healings

His Glory Revealed: Jesus Turns the Water into Wine

> **John 2:11**
>
> This, the first of His miraculous signs, Jesus performed at Cana in Galilee. He thus revealed His glory, and His disciples put their faith in Him.

Illustration:

Mel Tari, in Like a Mighty Wind, relates how this happened in the Indonesian revival. Many criticized the claims of this book. However, Mel Tari is a personal friend of Rolland Baker, and was in his wedding. He told Rolland, that instead of exaggeration, the accounts actually played down the supernatural because they knew the West couldn't accept them. They didn't tell all.

Glorification: Revelation and Faith to do the Works of the Father

It is implied here about the Father's glorification of Jesus that he was glorified by the words and works the Father gave him. He was glorified not just with words to speak to the people, but with the words about what to do, that is, with the revelation that creates the faith which produces the miraculous.

Jesus raises Lazarus from the dead.

At the Report that Lazarus was Sick, Looking Forward to the Miracle

> **John 8:54**
>
> Jesus replied, "If I glorify myself, my glory means nothing. My Father, whom you claim as your God, is the one who glorifies me.

> **John 11:4**
>
> When He heard this, Jesus said, "This sickness will not end in death. No, it is for God's glory so that God's Son may be glorified through it."

At the funeral of Lazarus after he died.

> **John 11:40**
>
> Then Jesus said, "Did I not tell you that if you believed, you would see the glory of God?"

People's unbelief after seeing Jesus doing miracles prophetically fulfills Isaiah seeing Jesus glory amidst Israel's hardness of heart.

> **John 12:37-41**
>
> Even after Jesus had done all these miraculous signs in their presence, they still would not believe in Him. This was to fulfill the word of Isaiah the prophet: "Lord, who has believed our message and to whom has the arm of the Lord been revealed?" For this reason they could not believe, because, as Isaiah says elsewhere: "He has blinded their eyes and deadened their hearts, so they can neither see with their eyes, nor understand with their hearts, nor turn - and I would heal them." Isaiah said this because he saw Jesus' glory and spoke about Him.

Supernatural Deeds Bring Glory to the Father

Believers doing the works in the name of Jesus.

> **John 14:13-14**
>
> And I will do whatever you ask in my name, so that the Son may bring glory to the Father. You may ask me for anything in my name, and I will do it.

By bearing much fruit.

We are so concerned in North America about fruit, usually the fruit of the Spirit listed in Galatians 5, but what about the fruit of John 15?

> **John 15:8**
>
> This is to my Father's glory, that you bear much fruit, showing yourselves to be my disciples.

Revelation is the source of faith for the miraculous and healing.

> **John 16:14**
>
> He will bring glory to me by taking from what is mine and making it known to you.

Jesus brought glory to the Father by completing the works given Him.

> **John 17:4-5**
>
> I have brought you glory on earth by completing the work you gave me to do. And now, Father, glorify me in your presence with the glory I had with you before the world began.
>
> **1 John 3:8b**
>
> ...The reason the Son of God appeared was to destroy the devil's work.

Implied, but strong in light of John 9:3, where Jesus healed the man born blind.

> **John 17:10**
>
> All I have is yours, and all you have is mine. And glory has come to me through them.
>
> **John 9:2-3**
>
> "Neither this man nor his parents sinned," said Jesus, "but this happened so that the works of God might be displayed in his life.

Implied: the glory is the power to work miracles, heal, and deliver.

> **John 17:20 & 22**
>
> I do not ask on behalf of these alone, but for those also who believe in Me through their word; I have given them the glory that you gave me, that they may be one as we are one.

Adam Clarke: And the glory which thou gavest me I have given them—That is, the power to work miracles, and to preach unadulterated truth, say some; but [Clarke's reasoning for the "but" in verse 20 is not having a view that God wanted all the saints to have access to this authority and power rather than just the disciples and apostles.] as our Lord is not here praying for the disciples, but for all those who should believe on him through their word, John 17:20, it is more natural to understand the passage thus. As Christ, according to his human nature, is termed the Son of God, he may be understood as saying: "I have communicated to all those who believe, or shall believe in me, the glorious privilege of becoming sons of God; that, being all adopted children of the same Father, they may abide in peace, love, and unity." For this reason it is said, Hebrews 2:11, Christ is not ashamed to call them brethren. However, our Lord may here, as in several other places, be using the past for the future; and the words may therefore be understood of the glory which they were to share with him in heaven.

The Apostle Paul – "Christ in you, the hope of glory" Empowers for Miracles

Paul speaks of the glory given to us through Christ Jesus to live a new life.

By strong inference, glory and power are used synonymously here by Paul.

> **Colossians 1:27**
>
> To them God has chosen to make known among the Gentiles the glorious riches of this mystery, which is Christ in you, the hope of glory.
>
> **Romans 5:2**
>
> Through whom we have gained access by faith into this grace in which we now stand. And we rejoice in the hope of the glory of God.
>
> **Romans 6:4**
>
> We were therefore buried with him through baptism into death in order that, just as Christ was raised from the dead through the glory of the Father, we too may live a new life.

By weak inference, but not if "glory" and "power" are used synonymously by Paul.

Adam Clarke, in his commentary wrote:

Raised up from the dead by the glory of the Father - from this we learn, that as it required the glory of the Father, that is, his glorious energy, to raise up from the grave the dead body of Christ, so it requires the same glorious energy to quicken the dead soul of a sinner, and enable him to walk in newness of life.

By weak inference, but not if "glory" and "power" are used synonymously by Paul.

This newness of life is not just for better morals. It is also a new power we have within us for doing the works of God. We have traditionally focused the redemption we have in Christ totally in the future, with only moral changes in this present life. I contend that this was not the understanding of the Early Church; it believed in a present power not only for moral change, but also for authority over demons, power over sickness and disease, and experiencing the reality of the spiritual gifts in their lives, and especially in the corporate life of the gathered congregations that made up the Church.

God Calls Us into His Kingdom and Glory

God calls us (present tense) now, not will call (future tense) us into His kingdom and glory.

> **1 Thessalonians 2:12**
>
> ...encouraging, comforting and urging you to live lives worthy of God, who calls you into His kingdom and glory.

God through the gospel to share in the glory of Christ.

> **2 Thessalonians 2:14**
>
> He called you to this through our gospel, that you might share in the glory of our Lord Jesus Christ.

Jesus, crowned with glory and honor, brings many sons to glory.

> **Hebrews 2:7-10**
>
> You made him a little lower than the angels; you crowned him with glory and honor and put everything under his feet. In putting everything under him, God left nothing that is not subject to him. Yet at present we do not see everything subject to him. But we see Jesus, who was made a little lower than the angels, now crowned with glory and honor because he suffered death, so that by the grace of God he might taste death for everyone. In bringing many sons to glory**, it was fitting that God, for whom and through whom everything exists, should make the author of their salvation perfect through suffering.

**Concerning the reference to our "glorified" bodies. Glorified bodies have been touched or produced by His glory, and have been changed, made fit for living in the presence of his glory. If that is what shall happen in the future, what will happen in the present if our bodies are touched by His glory? - healing and restoration.

Matthew Henry: (1.) In the choice of the end; and that was to bring many sons to glory in enjoying the glorious privileges of the gospel, and to future glory in heaven, which will be glory indeed, an exceeding eternal weight of glory.

The Bible Knowledge Commentary: 2:10. The author here continued to think of Psalm 8, as his reference to "everything" reveals (cf. Heb. 2:8). Thus the glory he mentioned here is also the glory referred to in the psalm, that is, the glory of dominion over the created order (cf. Heb. 2:78). Even the expression many sons is inspired by the psalmist's mention of "the Son of Man" and suggests that for the writer of Hebrews the messianic title Son of Man probably had a corporate aspect.

The Apostle Peter – The Spirit of Glory and Suffering

> **Matthew 17:1-5**
>
> After six days Jesus took with Him Peter, James and John the brother of James, and led them up a high mountain by themselves. There He was transfigured before them. His face shone like the sun, and His clothes became as white as the light. Just then there appeared before them Moses and Elijah, talking with Jesus. Peter said to Jesus, "Lord, it is good for us to be here. If you wish, I will put up three shelters – one for you, one for Moses and one for Elijah." While he was still speaking, a bright cloud enveloped them, and a voice from the cloud said, "This is My Son, whom I love; with Him I am well pleased. Listen to Him!"

Peter, Jesus' Transfiguration and the Cloud of Glory

> **2 Peter 1:16-18**
>
> We did not follow cleverly invented stories when we told you about the power and coming of our Lord Jesus Christ, but we were eyewitnesses of His majesty. For He received honor and glory from God the Father when the voice came to Him from the Majestic Glory, saying, "This is my Son, whom I love; with Him I am well pleased." We ourselves heard this voice that came from heaven when we were with Him on the sacred mountain.

Jesus' experience of manifested glory in His body that Peter witnessed was to prepare Him for the agony of the cross. Glory is not just for healing, but also to prepare for difficult times of persecution and suffering related to the mission of God, not suffering from disease and sickness.

The Spirit of Glory and of God Rests on the Persecuted

> **1 Peter 4:13-14**
>
> But rejoice that you participate in the sufferings of Christ, so that you may be overjoyed when His glory is revealed. If you are insulted because of the name of Christ, you are blessed, for the Spirit of glory and of God rests on you.

"Overjoyed when His glory is revealed" - Why limit this to only a future meaning, when it could also have a present meaning or a "soon meaning" in this life for the hearers of Peter's letter; especially, if they understood the connection between suffering persecution and moving in the power of His glory?

Closing Illustrations:

- Jamie Galloway in Curitiba, Brazil in the summer of 2003 was taken up to the third heaven and saw the glory cloud. That evening, his body was seen glowing with a glow about 2 inches around him, during which he experienced great power for healing.

- Gary Oates saw the glory of the Lord, and afterwards entered into a much greater anointing for healing. This happened on one of our trips to Volta Redonda, Brazil.

CHAPTER 17

HOW THIRSTY ARE YOU?

LESSON GOALS

1. To ask yourself the question: How thirsty am I?

2. To receive a powerful impartation of the Holy Spirit in response Jesus Christ's call to all who are thirsty to drink from the spring of the water of life!

INTRODUCTION

> **Revelation 21:6**
>
> He said to me: "It is done. I am the Alpha and the Omega, the Beginning and the End. To him who is thirsty I will give to drink without cost from the spring of the water of life.

In this session Randy Clark will be sharing testimony and stories to make you thirsty for more of God! The following passages are central to his sharing:

Revelation 21:1-6

Then I saw a new heaven and a new earth, for the first heaven and the first earth had passed away, and there was no longer any sea. I saw the Holy City, the new Jerusalem, coming down out of heaven from God, prepared as a bride beautifully dressed for her husband. And I heard a loud voice from the throne saying, "Now the dwelling of God is with men, and he will live with them. They will be his people, and God himself will be with them and be their God. He will wipe every tear from their eyes. There will be no more death or mourning or crying or pain, for the old order of things has passed away." He who was seated on the throne said, "I am making everything new!" Then he said, "Write this down, for these words are trustworthy and true." He said to me: "It is done. I am the Alpha and the Omega, the Beginning and the End. To him who is thirsty I will give to drink without cost from the spring of the water of life.

1 Corinthians 12:13

For we were all baptized by one Spirit into one body—whether Jews or Greeks, slave or free— and we were all given the one Spirit to drink.

John 7:37-39

On the last and greatest day of the Feast, Jesus stood and said in a loud voice, "If anyone is thirsty, let him come to me and drink. Whoever believes in me, as the Scripture has said, streams of living water will flow from within him." By this he meant the Spirit, whom those who believed in him were later to receive. Up to that time the Spirit had not been given, since Jesus had not yet been glorified

IMPARTATION

This session of our Healing School is an opportunity for you to drink freely from the spring of the water of life! Come thirsty and expecting!

NOTES

NOTES

NOTES

NOTES